First World War
and Army of Occupation
War Diary
France, Belgium and Germany

7 INDIAN (MEERUT) DIVISION
Headquarters, Branches and Services
Commander Royal Artillery
1 April 1915 - 30 April 1915

WO95/3933/4

The Naval & Military Press Ltd
www.nmarchive.com
Published in association with The National Archives

Published by

The Naval & Military Press Ltd

Unit 10 Ridgewood Industrial Park,

Uckfield, East Sussex,

TN22 5QE England

Tel: +44 (0) 1825 749494

www.naval-military-press.com

www.nmarchive.com

This diary has been reprinted in facsimile from the original. Any imperfections are inevitably reproduced and the quality may fall short of modern type and cartographic standards.

© Crown Copyright
Images reproduced by permission of The National Archives, London, England, 2015.

Contents

Document type	Place/Title	Date From	Date To
Heading	Meerut Division H.Q. Div Artillery From 1st to 30th April 1915		
Heading	War Diary With Appendices Head Quarters Divisional Artillery Meerut Division From 1st April 1915 30th April 1915		
War Diary	Veille Chapelle	01/04/1915	04/04/1915
War Diary	Fosse	05/04/1915	30/04/1915
Miscellaneous	A Form Messages And Signals		
Miscellaneous	CRA		
Miscellaneous	Copy of A Memo No.G 483 dated 2nd April 1915 Received from Indian Corps	02/04/1915	02/04/1915
Operation(al) Order(s)	Operation Order No.26 By Lieutenant General Sir Charles Anderson K.C.B. Commanding Meerut Division	09/04/1915	09/04/1915
Miscellaneous	March Table		
Diagram etc	Diagram		
Operation(al) Order(s)	Operation Order No.15 By Brigadier General R. St. C. Lecky Commanding Royal Artillery Meerut Division	10/04/1915	10/04/1915
Miscellaneous	March Table		
Miscellaneous	Amendments to Meerut Divisional Artillery Operation Order No.15 dated 10-4-15	10/04/1915	10/04/1915
Miscellaneous	Tactical Progress Report	15/04/1915	15/04/1915
Miscellaneous	Tactical Progress Report	16/04/1915	16/04/1915
Miscellaneous	Tactical Progress Report	17/04/1915	17/04/1915
Miscellaneous	Tactical Progress Report	18/04/1915	18/04/1915
Miscellaneous	Appendix 139	19/04/1915	19/04/1915
Miscellaneous	Tactical Progress Report	19/04/1915	19/04/1915
Operation(al) Order(s)	Operation Order No.27 By Lieutenant-General Sir C.A. Anderson K.C.B. Commanding Meerut Division	20/04/1915	20/04/1915
Miscellaneous	March Table		
Miscellaneous	Tactical Progress Report	20/04/1915	20/04/1915
Miscellaneous	Tactical Progress Report	21/04/1915	21/04/1915
Miscellaneous	Tactical Progress Report	22/04/1915	22/04/1915
Operation(al) Order(s)	Operation Order No.16 By Brigadier General R.St.C. Lecky R.A. C.R.A. Meerut Division	23/04/1915	23/04/1915
Miscellaneous	Tactical Progress Report	23/04/1915	23/04/1915
Miscellaneous	A Form Messages And Signals		
Miscellaneous	Tactical Progress Report	24/04/1915	24/04/1915
Miscellaneous	A Form Messages And Signals		
Miscellaneous	Tactical Progress Report	25/04/1915	25/04/1915
Miscellaneous	A Form Messages And Signals		
Miscellaneous	Meerut Divisional Artillery	25/04/1915	25/04/1915
Miscellaneous	Tactical Progress Report	28/04/1915	28/04/1915
Operation(al) Order(s)	Operation Order No.28 By Lieut: General Sir C.A. Anderson K.C.B. Commanding Meerut Division	26/04/1915	26/04/1915
Miscellaneous	March Table		
Miscellaneous	G-43/49 Head Quarters Meerut Division	27/04/1915	27/04/1915
Miscellaneous	Tactical Progress Report	27/04/1915	27/04/1915
Operation(al) Order(s)	Operation Order No.17 By Brigadier General R. St. C. Lecky R.A. C.R.A. Meerut Division	27/04/1915	27/04/1915

Miscellaneous	Instructions for Moves ? Group Meerut Divisional Artillery 29th April 1915	28/04/1915	28/04/1915
Miscellaneous	A Form Messages And Signals		
Miscellaneous	Tactical Progress Report	28/04/1915	28/04/1915
Miscellaneous	Tactical Progress Report	29/04/1915	29/04/1915
Miscellaneous	Tactical Progress Report	30/04/1915	30/04/1915

Meerut Division

H. Q. Div. Artillery.

From 1st To 30th April 1915

121/5504

Bound No 65

MC 6/5

WAR DIARY
with appendices.

Head Quarters. Divisional Artillery Meerut Division.

From 1st April 1915 To 30. April 1915

Army Form C.

WAR DIARY VOLUME IX
or
INTELLIGENCE SUMMARY.

(Erase heading not required.)

Instructions regarding War Diaries and Intelligence Summaries are contained in F.S. Regs., Part II. and the Staff Manual respectively. Title pages will be prepared in manuscript.

Hour, Date, Place	Summary of Events and Information	Remarks and references to Appendices
1st April 1915. VIEILLE CHAPELLE	RESTING.	MM9
2nd April 1915. VIEILLE CHAPELLE	RESTING. MEERUT Division Nº Q.C.577 & G.370/2 received regarding 9th and 13th Brigades R.F.A. rejoining MEERUT Division on night 3rd/4th April.	* Appendix 130 MM9 *Appendix 131
3rd April 1915. VIEILLE CHAPELLE	RESTING. MEERUT Division Nº 370/3 received giving details of moves of 9th and 13th Brigades R.F.A.	Appendix 132 MM9
4th April 1915. VIEILLE CHAPELLE	RESTING. 9th Brigade R.F.A. proceeded into billets at BUSNES during the night 3rd/4th April. Captain P.G. ROBINSON, R.A. Staff Captain R.A. MEERUT Division proceeded on short leave to England.	MM9
5th April 1915. FOSSE	RESTING. 13th Brigade R.F.A. proceeded into billets at LA BRASSERIE during night 4th/5th April.	MM9
12 noon do ...	Headquarters Divisional Artillery MEERUT Division moved into billets at FOSSE. Brigadier General R. St. C. LECKY, G.O.C. R.A. MEERUT Division and Lieutenant F.N. MASON MACFARLANE, R.A. Orderly Officer and A.D.C. to G.O.C., R.A. returned from short leave in England.	
6th April 1915. FOSSE	RESTING	MM9
7th April 1915. FOSSE	RESTING	MM9
8th April 1915. FOSSE	RESTING	MM9

Army Form C. 2118.

WAR DIARY
or
INTELLIGENCE SUMMARY.
(Erase heading not required.)

Hour, Date, Place	Summary of Events and Information	Remarks and references to Appendices
9th April 1915. FOSSE	RESTING. MEERUT Division Operation Order Nº 26 received. The MEERUT Division are about to take over that portion of the Line now held by the LAHORE and 1st Divisions — up to and including the ORCHARD about 400 yds S.W. of PORT ARTHUR.	* Appendix 133 WR.P.
10th April 1915. FOSSE	RESTING. Operation Order Nº 15 by G.O.C., R.A. issued.	* Appendix 134 WR.P.
11th April 1915. FOSSE	RESTING. Captain P.G. ROBINSON, R.A. Staff Capt. R.A. MEERUT Division returned from short leave in England.	WR.P.
12th April 1915. FOSSE	The following moves were carried out in accordance with the March Table issued with Operation Order Nº 15:— 28th Battery R.F.A. BUSNES to ETON ROAD, PONT du HEM (M 15 c 3.3) 1 Sect 4th " " LA BRASSERIE to CROIX BARBEE (M 20 c 9.1) 1 Sect 8th " " " do do (M 31 7.8.7)	WR.P.
13th April 1915. FOSSE	1 Sect 7th Battery R.F.A. RUE du VINAGE to CROIX BARBEE (M 26 c 7.5) 20th Battery R.F.A. BUSNES to RUGBY ROAD (M 21 Z 6.7) 2nd Battery R.F.A. LA BRASSERIE to LORETTO ROAD (M 33 a 9.9) 14th Battery R.F.A. } RIEZ du VINAGE to CROIX BARBEE { M 31 d 4.9 64th Battery R.F.A. } { M 33 a 2.3 1 Sect 5th How Bty R.F.A. ROBECQ to RUGBY ROAD. (M 22 d 0.3)	WR.P.
14th April 1915. FOSSE	19th Battery R.F.A. BUSNES to PONT du HEM (M 21 a 3.3) 2 Sect 7th Battery R.F.A. RIEZ du VINAGE to CROIX BARBEE (M 26 c 5.5) 2 Sect 14th Battery R.F.A. LA BRASSERIE to ROUGE CROIX – HARROW ROAD (M 20 c 9.1) 2 Sects 8th Battery R.F.A. do to CROIX BARBEE (M 31 7.8.7) 4th Bde R.F.A. Ammn Col RIEZ du VINAGE to R 19 a 2.10. 7/13th Bde do BUSNES to R 12 c 5.4 8/13th Bde do LA BRASSERIE to R 32 Z 8.6 13th Bde do ROBECQ to LES LOBES	WR.P.

Forms/C.2118/190
(9 29 6) W 4141-483 100,000 9/14 HWV

Army Form C. 2118.

WAR DIARY
or
INTELLIGENCE SUMMARY.
(Erase heading not required.)

Instructions regarding War Diaries and Intelligence Summaries are contained in F.S. Regs., Part II. and the Staff Manual respectively. Title pages will be prepared in manuscript.

Hour, Date, Place	Summary of Events and Information	Remarks and references to Appendices
12 noon 15th April 1915. FOSSE.	The G.O.C., R.A. MEERUT Division assumed command of the Artillery on this line from the G.O.C.'s R.A. 1st and LAHORE Divisions.	
12.15. p.m. do.	40th How: Battery fired a few rounds shrapnel at enemy front trenches near point 130, also at working party in rear of fire trenches near this point.	
12.45 p.m. do.	4th the Battery was shelled by 4.2" Howitzer - fuze set at 46 - only one shell fell very near the battery.	x Appendix 134.
2.25 p.m. do.	German aeroplane seen proceeding Northwards - was engaged by anti-aircraft guns and it then made off in a N.N.E. direction. It was flying very high.	
4. p.m. do.	Flashes of hostile battery firing on RUE BACQUEROT from ridge near HAUTE POMMERAU. During the day all batteries continued registration and the various points. The following moves were carried out in accordance with Operation Order No. 15:- 30th How: Battery (less 1 section) ROBECQ to ST. VAAST (M 32 d 8.8). 2 Section 57th How. Battery ROBECQ to RUGBY Road (M 22 a 2.3). Tonight the section of 59th How Battery at M 22 d 0.3 moved to new position at M 22 a 2.3 owing to there being insufficient cover at former place. Copy of Tactical Progress Report is attached	x Appendix 135.

Army Form C. 2118.

WAR DIARY
and
INTELLIGENCE SUMMARY.
(Erase heading not required.)

Instructions regarding War Diaries and Intelligence Summaries are contained in F.S. Regs., Part II. and the Staff Manual respectively. Title pages will be prepared in manuscript.

Hour, Date, Place	Summary of Events and Information	Remarks and references to Appendices
4.45.a.m. 16th April 1915 FOSSE.	8th Battery fired 3 rounds registering on road S 11 c 4'4.	
8.a.m. do.	Enemy's 4'2" How: fired 12 rounds on support trenches M 29 b 4'3.	
9.a.m. do.	Enemy's 4'2" How: fired a few rounds on support trenches M 29 d 4'5.	
9.20 to 9.30 do.	Enemy's 4'2" How: fired on trenches M 29 b 8'2.	
10 to 11a.m. do.	Enemy shelled our fire trenches in rear of point 62 with field gun— probably from FERME du BIEZ.	
10.15.a.m. do.	Enemy's 4'2" How: fired on footpath running from MIN (M 22 d 4'0).	
10 to 10.30 do.	Redoubt of 2nd Siege Battery (M 23 o) was shelled by enemy's 4'2" How: doing good practice.	
10.30 to 10.50 do.	Enemy's 4'2" How: fired on Redoubt M 23 c.	x Appendix 134
12 noon do.	7th Battery fired 3 rounds at German trenches at point 130.	
1.p.m. do.	O.C. 30th How: Battery reported RUE du BOIS shelled.	
1.5.p.m. do.	7th Battery O.P. shelled at one minute intervals between rounds— 2 direct hits on house— battery not located. This O.P. was again shelled by German Heavy Battery at 4.p.m.	
2.5.p.m. do.	Intermittent shelling of our trenches in S 10 b by field battery and a 5'9" How: — not located.	
2.30.pm.m do.	Enemy's 4'2" How: fired on line M 29 & 5'5 to M 29 & 8'10. This battery, which was firing during the best part of the morning, was probably registering— not located. Enemy field gun fired 10 H.E. on support trenches western edge M 29 d.	
3.5.p.m. do.	Enemy observed rebuilding parapet 264.	
3.p.m. do.	PIPSQUEAK fired 4 rounds into M 35 b 0'5, and just previous to this a few rounds in vicinity of 2nd Battery's gun position.	
3.26.p.m. do.	14th Battery registered on parapet 20 yards E. of LA BASSEE Road— one direct hit obtained.	
4.p.m. do.	House at M 32 d 8'2 was shelled by 8" How: — 3 direct hits— battery approximately located by sound as firing from T 2 c.	
4.15 to 4.30 do.	About 10 to 15 5'9" high explosive How: shell fell about 200 to 300 yards in front of 30th How: Battery position— pieces went into battery— no casualties.	
4. p.m. do.	House at M 32 d 7'4 shelled by PIPSQUEAK.	

Army Form C. 2118.

WAR DIARY
or
INTELLIGENCE SUMMARY.
(Erase heading not required.)

Instructions regarding War Diaries and Intelligence Summaries are contained in F.S. Regs., Part II. and the Staff Manual respectively. Title pages will be prepared in manuscript.

Hour, Date, Place	Summary of Events and Information	Remarks and references to Appendices
5.p.m. 16th April 1915. FOSSE.	Enemy shelled vicinity of PORT ARTHUR with Howitzer and PIPSQUEAK from S. of BOIS du BIEZ. 57th How: Battery shelled SNIPER'S House (263) firing 16 lyddite and 4 shrapnel. Practice not unsatisfcatory. * For further information see Tactical Progress Report dated 16th April 1915.	+ Appendix 134 * Appendix 136.

Army Form C. 2118.

WAR DIARY
or
INTELLIGENCE SUMMARY.
(*Erase heading not required.*)

Instructions regarding War Diaries and Intelligence Summaries are contained in F.S. Regs., Part II. and the Staff Manual respectively. Title pages will be prepared in manuscript.

Hour, Date, Place	Summary of Events and Information	Remarks and references to Appendices
17th April 1915, ...	Snipers very quiet on front during night 16th/17th. Further registration on more distant points was carried out during the day.	
3.4.a.m. do............	Bomb guns active opposite Section E. Infantry reported 2 of these guns in enemy's trench S.W. of points 203 and 204.	+ Appendix 154
6.45.a.m. do............	German field howitzer fired 8 shell at Brewery at NEUVE CHAPELLE— battery not located.	
6.50 to 7.a.m. do............	PIPSQUEAK was active at MIN Farm.	
7.5.a.m. do............	Enemy 4'2" How: shelled support trenches M 28 b 5'5 to M 28 b 7'8. 3 rounds fired.	
7.15.a.m. do............	Enemy 4'2" How: shelled support trenches in M 29 c 8'7 — probably from direction of N 32 d.	
7.25 to 8.5a.m.do......	PIPSQUEAK active along the RUE de BACQUEROT.	
7.30 to) do............	Billet of 57th How: Battery used as Heavy Battery Observing Station (M 21 d 10'3) was shelled by about 50 to 60 H.E. shell, 12 to 14 of which were direct hits on the buildings. Shell were apparently from a 4" gun and a light field gun intermixed. Shell groove in front of farm gave magnetic bearing of 125°.	
8.50.a.m.)		
8.5.a.m. do............	German field gun fired a few rounds on trenches at point 205 - not located.	
10.5.a.m. do............	Enemy 4'2" How: active on M 28 d from direction of HAUTE POMMEREAU.	
10.15.a.m. do............	Observing Officer 20th Battery reported enemy's field guns firing occasional rounds into area M 29 a - not located.	
10.55.a.m. do............	Enemy 4'2" How: shelled out-trenches about M 35 a 7'7 from S 6 b 5'5.	
11,15.a.m. do............	German field How: firing over NEUVE CHAPELLE from behind BOIS du BIEZ.	
11.30.a.m. do............	Enemy 4'2" How: shelled road M 35 a 7'0 to M 35 c 7'7.	
12 noon do............	German field gun shelled road about M 15 c 8'7 for about 20 minutes— probably due to wagons moving along that road at the time. Field battery fired on M 15 d from direction of N 32 d.	
1.30.p.m. do............	German field battery opened fire; but ceased at once on 28th Battery engaging N 31 b 5'0.	
2.p.m. do............	German battery shelled trenches of "C" Sub-section. 7th battery fired on trenches opposite.	

(3-29 6) W4141-433 100,000 9/14 H W V Forms/C. 2118/10

Army Form C. 2118.

WAR DIARY
or
INTELLIGENCE SUMMARY.
(Erase heading not required.)

Instructions regarding War Diaries and Intelligence Summaries are contained in F.S. Regs., Part II. and the Staff Manual respectively. Title pages will be prepared in manuscript.

Hour, Date, Place	Summary of Events and Information	Remarks and references to Appendices
2.p.m. to 17th April 1915.. FOSSE.		
4.p.m.)		
3.15.p.m. do........	20th Battery registered some distant points, also fired in N 31 d 5'8 and SNIPER's House in M 30 c 8'8. 8th Battery fired at communication trench at S 11 a 5'2 where some germans were seen moving.	
3.20.p.m. do........	2nd Siege Battery registered FERME du BIEZ-2nd round direct hit causing a big conflagration.	
4.30.p.m. do........	At request of Infantry 57th How: Battery fired on a small White House at point 259. Though the house was not actually destroyed its colour is now yellow.	+ appendix 152
4.50.p.m. do........	German How: battery fired on CRESCENT trench- apparently from S 17 a.	
5.5 to 5.17p.m. do....	Continuous crackle was heard at FERME du BIEZ for 12 minutes-thought that S.A.A. store there had been destroyed.	
5.15.p.m. do........	57th How: Battery fired on MIN du PIETRE obtaining 1 direct hit on the chimney with percussion and 2 rounds of lyddite as close as they could have been without actually knocking down the chimney. This chimney is without doubt used for observing and sniping on communicating trenches. * Further information will be found in the Progress Report of today.	* Appendix 137.

Army Form C. 2118.

WAR DIARY
or
INTELLIGENCE SUMMARY.
(Erase heading not required.)

Hour, Date, Place	Summary of Events and Information	Remarks and references to Appendices
2.a.m. to 4.a.m. } 18th April 1915 FOSSE.	O.C. 2nd Siege Battery reported heavy rifle and machine gun fire heaviest from direction of MIN du PIETRE, accompanied with occasional Artillery fire.	
7.15.a.m. do	German field gun fired 3 rounds 200 yds short of 28th Battery- all 3 were blind.	
7.50.a.m. do	Hostile aeroplane sighted at bearing 115° flying high but out of range turned in N.N.E. direction.	
9.14.a.m. do	Hostile aeroplane MORANE (German) flying high bearing 250°, engaged by Archibald and turned in N.N.E. direction.	
9.50.a.m. do	Hostile aeroplane AVIATIC flying high bearing 200°, was engaged by our Archibald and turned in Easterly direction.	
10.20 to 11.40.a.m. } do	German field gun (reported yesterday as being in N 31.b 5'0 now thought to be more N.E. of that) opened fire on cross roads M 22 b 9'5 (RUE BACQUEROT), then searched up to 28th Battery position and across road at M 15 a 9'5. About 11.a.m. German 4" gun joined in and fired on the latter vicinity. It is thought that these 2 batteries must be the same which shelled 57th How:Battery billet from direction N 31.b 5'0, both direction fired from and fuzes picked up which correspond. 4th Brigade R.F.A. fired on communication trench near point 139.	×Appendix 137
2.p.m. to 3.30.p.m. } do		
2.30.p.m. do	20th Battery fired on enemy's trenches in "G" Section and working parties.	
3.10.p.m. do	Small Howitzer fired 3 shell on RUE de BACQUEROT in M 22 c. 8th Battery opened fire on enemy working party in a trench about S 11 a 3'2- enemy fled.	
3.30.p.m. do	Batteries of 4th Brigade R.F.A. fired at point 63.	×
4.25.p.m. do	Batteries of 4th Brigade R.F.A. fired a few rounds on German trenches to keep down hostile fire on our aeroplane.	
4.45.p.m. do	Batteries of 4th Brigade R.F.A. fired at 150 yds N.E. of point 51 behind fire trench.	
6.10.p.m. do	14th Battery R.F.A. fired on party of men going down communicating trench at point 57.	×
6.30.p.m. do	Enemy fired 6 rounds from light howitzer at cross roads M 35 a 7'3- not located.	
	Further information will be found in Progress Report attached.*	* Appendix 138

Army Form C. 2118.

WAR DIARY
or
INTELLIGENCE SUMMARY.
(Erase heading not required.)

Instructions regarding War Diaries and Intelligence Summaries are contained in F.S. Regs, Part II. and the Staff Manual respectively. Title pages will be prepared in manuscript.

Hour, Date, Place	Summary of Events and Information	Remarks and references to Appendices
12.30.a.m. 19th April 1915. FOSSE.	8th Battery fired on enemy's trenches to retaliate for those of 2nd 8th Gurkhas being shelled.	
5.15.a.m.	PIPSQUEAK fired a few rounds at our trenches.	
8.20.a.m.	Observing station of 4th Bde R.F.A. in NEUVE CHAPELLE was shelled by 4'2" how: from direction of S 6 b 5'5. Brewery at NEUVE CHAPELLE shelled- telephone wires cut.	↳appendix 154
8.44.a.m.	7th Battery observation post shelled.	
8.45.a.m.	PIPSQUEAK active from S 17 a on our trenches- 14th Battery fired a few rounds and firing ceased. Batteries of R.A. Centre Group fired on house near point 125 thought to be German Observation Post.	
9.45.a.m.	Batteries of R.A. Centre Group fired on Observation house in S 5 d 10'9.	
10.45.a.m.	" " registered supposed battery position	
10.47.a.m.	" " bearing 140, was out	
10.57.a.m.	Hostile aeroplane sighted,flying high,magnetic bearing 350°, was out of range and turned due East.	
11.a.m.	Hostile aeroplane sighted, flying high, magnetic bearing N.N.E.	
11.15.a.m.	CRESCENT trench shelled by PIPSQUEAK.	
11.25.a.m.	German field battery fire,one shrapnel near ROUGE CROIX. 20th Battery reported one heavy H.E. fell near NEUVE CHAPELLE and some rounds near houses at M 23 b 4'3.	
11.30.a.m.	57th How:Battery fired on point 203 where working parties were reported making emplacements for "bomb" guns. CROIX BARBEE shelled by light howitzer- 3 rounds.	
11.50.a.m.	German 4'2" How: shelled our trenches in F section. 12 to 15 Germans noticed in Redoubt S 10 d 5'8 who commenced bombing our trenches in reply to our bombing. 2nd Siege Battery fired 3 rds H.L. no hit but near enough to make them stop. Field battery also fired 2 or 3 rounds and brought them to ground. Smoke from the bomb thrower when fired was distinctly visible.	
11.55.a.m.	German 4'2" How: shelled locality M 21 d 8'2 firing 5 rounds- direction thought to be from M 31 b 5'8.	
12.15.p.m.	PIPSQUEAK from direction of AUBERS fired 4 shell at 57th billet.	
1.20.p.m.	28th Battery fired registering rounds on road running S.E. from MIN du PIETRE.	

Army Form C. 2118.

WAR DIARY
or
INTELLIGENCE SUMMARY.
(Erase heading not required.)

Instructions regarding War Diaries and Intelligence Summaries are contained in F.S. Regs., Part II. and the Staff Manual respectively. Title pages will be prepared in manuscript.

Hour, Date, Place	Summary of Events and Information	Remarks and references to Appendices
1.45.p.m. 19th April 1915...	CRESCENT trench shelled by enemy's 5"9 Howitzer.	
2.20.p.m. do............	Batteries of R.A. Centre Group fired at working party at point 63. ✗	
3.p.m. do............	German field gun from about S 12 c fired a few rounds into NEUVE CHAPELLE.	
3.5.p.m. do............	Batteries of R.A. Centre Group put 3 good rounds into strong working party at fire trench S 11 b. PIPSQUEAK fired 6 rounds on the MIN M 22 d 2'4, obtaining one direct hit— thought to be from direction N 25 and same battery that fired at 12.15.p.m. One German field gun from about T 7 fired into NEUVE CHAPELLE. ✗	✗ Appendix 134.
3.20.p.m. do............	Batteries of R.A. Centre Group fired at working party at point 63.	
3.15.p.m. do............	German howitzer battery from direction of N 31 c (probably same battery that opened fire at 11.50.a.m. and reported from N 31 b) shelled our reserve trenches in the vicinity of M 34 b 4'7.	
3.35.p.m. do............	German battery fired 5 H.E. shell at cross roads at M 15 c 7'7.	
5.15.p.m. do............	Batteries of R.A. Centre Group fired a few rounds into house S.W. of point 125 ✗ where enemy were seen to be sniping from.	
7.p.m. do............	Enemy fired 4 large bombs into salient trench from point 204— 2nd Battery fired 2 rounds on this point and bombing ceased. = ✗	
	Report on wire entanglements etc by 30th Howitzer Battery is attached.	* Appendix 139. # Appendix 140.
	Further information will be found in the Daily Progress Report.	[signature]
	Re techn. 5th Siege Battery joined from IV Corps and rest into position at M 26 c 3.0.	

Forms/C. 2118/10

Army Form C. 2118.

WAR DIARY
or
INTELLIGENCE SUMMARY.
(Erase heading not required.)

Instructions regarding War Diaries and Intelligence Summaries are contained in F.S. Regs., Part II. and the Staff Manual respectively. Title pages will be prepared in manuscript.

Hour, Date, Place	Summary of Events and Information	Remarks and references to Appendices
4.10.a.m. 20th April 1915. FOSSE.	28th Battery shelled wire in front of German trench in "H" Section.	
4.30.a.m. do......	19th Battery fired on wire of German trenches.	
4.40.a.m. do......	20th Battery fired 6 rounds on German trenches in "G" Section.	
5.30.a.m. do......	2nd Battery shelled wire in front of German trenches in "E" Section.	
8.15 to 8.45.a.m. do......	57th How: Battery registered house at point 186. German Howitzer shelled 28th Battery O.P. and houses in locality- direction unknown.	
9.a.m. do......	57th How: Battery fired a few rounds at MOULIN du PIETRE.	
9.45.a.m. do......	German field gun shelled support trenches in "G" Section and communicating trenches in M 29 c - probably from direction N 31 b 6'.9'. Batteries of R.A. Centre Group registered fire trench E, of point 53.	×Appendix 154
10.a.m. do......	German 5'9" Howitzer shelled CHAPIGNY.	
11.a.m. do......	How: and 66th Battery of R.A. Centre Group fired on point 66- this was repeated at 12 noon.	
11.15.a.m. do......	German field gun shelled communication trench in "E" Section.	
12.20.p.m. do......	German field gun fired 9 rounds on vicinity M 22 a 1'.2- same battery that shelled at 11,15.a.m. Batteries of R.A. Centre Group fired on large working parties between points 130 and 131.	
12.35.p.m. do......	German howitzer fired 6 rounds across road at M 15 a 9'2.	
12.55.p.m. do......	PIPSQUEAK shelled RUE de BACQUEROT M 22 b from direction LES MOTTES Fme. Batteries of the R.A. Centre Group registered the FERME du BIEZ.	
1.30.p.m. do......	Enemy 5'9" How: shells fell near position of 57th How: Battery.	
1.30 to 2.30.p.m. do......	Headquarters 2nd Siege Battery shelled.	
1.43.p.m. do......	Enemy shelled St VAAST and RICHEBOURG- about 25 shell.	
1.45.p.m. do......	German Sausage Balloons seen, true bearing 144° 30' from M 31 b 9'.7.	
1.55.p.m. do......	German 4'2" How fired 5 H.E. shell near the MIN M 22 d.	
2.5.p.m. do......	German 4'2" How: (apparently same as fired at 1.55.p.m.) fired one percussion at cross roads M 15 c 7'7 and one H.E. 300 yds in front of 28th Battery position and one H.E.S. of the MIN.	
8.10.p.m. do......	Same battery shelled cross roads at M 15 c 7'7 and cross roads at PONT du HEM.	

Army Form C. 2118.

WAR DIARY
or
INTELLIGENCE SUMMARY.
(Erase heading not required.)

Instructions regarding War Diaries and Intelligence Summaries are contained in F.S. Regs., Part II. and the Staff Manual respectively. Title pages will be prepared in manuscript.

Hour, Date, Place	Summary of Events and Information	Remarks and references to Appendices
2.30.p.m. 30th April 1915. FOSSE.	"MOTHER" destroyed MOULIN du PIETRE chimney.	
2.35.p.m. do......	20th Battery fired 5 rounds on enemy's 2nd line trenches.	
3.p.m. do......	57th How: Battery registered house at point 186. 2nd Battery reported believed to have seen flashes at T 2 d 2˙2 ARRET and M 27 d 8˙8. Hostile aeroplane AVIATIK, bearing 125°, high, turned E, to bearing 90° came over three times, was engaged and 83 rounds fired at it- last seen 4.p.m. travelling S.E.	
3.10.p.m. do......	2nd Battery registered on point 204, reported as exact position of "bomb" guns. The point is 85 yds W, of and 15 yds S. of centre of 204.	
3.30.p.m. do......	2nd Battery fired 4 rounds on house E. of 204.	
3.55.p.m. do......	XXX 57th How: Battery registered LES MOTTES Fme. Hostile aeroplane AVIATIK, high, bearing 103°, engaged 21 rounds, turned N.E. 7th Division R.A. reported 2 houses each side of point 260 and haystack between 252 and 260 used by snipers and enfilading our trenches- 57th 20th and 28th Batteries were ordered to fire on these points daily.	→ Appendix 139.
4.p.m. do......	8th Battery fired at working party in trench at S 11 a 3˙2-Germans wearing new dark blue uniforms some with light blue collars.	
4.15.p.m. do......	Batteries of R.A. Centre Group fired on enemy's Infantry who were firing at our aeroplanes. 2 German Gausage Balloons seen, true bearing 158° and 198° from M 31 b 9˙7.	[handwritten note: Enemy behaving 1 set large Battery firing from IX Corps and not with position at M26 c 3 0]
4.50.p.m. do......	Hostile aeroplane AVIATIK bearing 105°, high, engaged with 16 rounds turned in S.E. direction.	
5.p.m. do......	8th Battery fired at Distillery and obtained 2 direct hits.	
5.15.p.m. do......	Hostile aeroplane AVIATIK, high bearing 125°, out of range, turned N.E.	
5.30.p.m. do......	57th How: Battery shelled house at point 252. 2nd Battery fired 8 rounds at house at point 260.	
5.45.p.m. do......	5˙9 How: shelled on vicinity of 57th How: Battery M 21 d- firing 3 rds.	
5.55.p.m. do......	Hostile aeroplane, AVIATIK, high, bearing 58°, turned N.E., out of range.	
6.p.m. do......	German Howitzer shelled vicinity M 15 d 2˙4.	
6. p.m. do......	Hostile aeroplane FOKKER, high, bearing 0°, one rd. fired, out of range, turned N.E. *Motor Gun Section order No 27 received.	* Appendix 140(a).
6.45.p.m. do......	Batteries of R.A. Centre Group fired at enemy in house at point 121. Further information will be found in daily Tactical Progress Report.*	* Appendix 141.

Army Form C. 2118.

WAR DIARY
or
INTELLIGENCE SUMMARY.
(Erase heading not required.)

Instructions regarding War Diaries and Intelligence Summaries are contained in F. S. Regs., Part II. and the Staff Manual respectively. Title pages will be prepared in manuscript.

Hour, Date, Place	Summary of Events and Information	Remarks and references to Appendices
=12.30.a.m. 21st April 1915 FOSSE.	Enemy bombed trenches in "F" Section-19th Battery replied with 2 rds- and bombing ceased.	
4.30.a.m.	28th Battery fired 3 rounds on wire in front of german trenches.	
5.a.m.	Enemy fired 2 bombs on our advance post at point 196 from behind trench between 204× and 146× 2nd Battery replied with 2 rounds and bombing ceased.	
5.30.a.m. do.........	Batteries of R.A. Centre Group fired on houses near 51.	
6.10.a.m. do.........	20th Battery shelled enemy's trenches and wire in "G" Section.	
6.25.a.m. do.........	2nd Battery shelled wire in front of enemy's trenches between points 146× and 204.	
	Infantry reported movement during the night about 204 and heavy firing from direction of YPRES.	
8.8.m to 9.30.a.m. do......... 8.30 a.m. do.........	20th Battery fired 3 rounds on sniper's haystack at point 260. Enemy shelled houses in NEUVE CHAPELLE including Brewery with 5'9", 4'2" How: and PIPSQUEAK, also shelled these places at intervals during the day. 2 telephonists of 44th Battery wounded.	× Appendix - 1324
8.45.a.m. do.........	Batteries of R.A. Centre Group fired on enemy's infantry who were watching German shell falling in NEUVE CHAPELLE.	
10.17.a.m. do.........	German heavy howitzer shelled LA BASSEE Road S. of PONT du HEM from direction of AUBERS.	
10.20.a.m. do.........	"Wooley Bear" fired on reserve trenches at M 35 a from direction of HAUTE POMMEREAU.	
10.40 to 10.50.a.m. do.....	German 6" Howitzer shelled near road M 27 b and d, apparently trying to hit tall house in M 27 b 4.2.	
10.50 to 11.4.a.m. do.........	German field battery fired on main road S. of ROUGE CROIX.	
11.a.m. do.........	8th Battery registered trench from V 6× to S 11 c 1'8.	
11 to 11.30.a.m.do.........	3 or 4 howitzer shell fell near 44th Battery.	
11.30.a.m. do.........	Some PIPSQUEAK shell fell near 8th Battery O.P.	
11.45.a.m. do.........	Batteries of R.A. Centre Group fired at working party at point 63.×	× 63 & 66.
12.30.p.m. do.........	Batteries of R.A. centre Group fired at working party between pts 63 & 66.	
12.50.p.m. do.........	19th Battery shelled trenches near point×204 to stop bombing. BAREILLY Brigade asked for fire on point 204 by heavy artillery—57th Howitzer Battery ordered to take it on.	
7.50.p.m. do.........	28th Battery shelled point 260×and MOULIN du PIETRE.	

Army Form C. 2118.

WAR DIARY
or
INTELLIGENCE SUMMARY.
(Erase heading not required.)

Instructions regarding War Diaries and Intelligence Summaries are contained in F. S. Regs., Part II. and the Staff Manual respectively. Title pages will be prepared in manuscript.

Hour, Date, Place	Summary of Events and Information	Remarks and references to Appendices
2.10.p.m. 21st April 1915. FOSSE.	57th How: Battery shelled point 204 and parapet between 204 and 146 as ordered, obtaining 3 direct hits on house at point 204.	
2.15.p.m. do........	House at ROUGE CROIX was shelled and set on fire by German 4'2" How:.	
2.25.p.m. do........	66th Battery fired 14 rounds in cooperation with Heavies at points 124 and 125 effect good.	
3.30.p.m. do........	Enemy shelled house at M 32 d 8'2 with 5'9". Batteries of R.A. Centre Group fired at party of Germans in communicating trench behind point 130.	+ Appendix 137
3.57..p.m. do........	Batteries of R.A. Centre Group fired at party of Germans in fire trench near point 51.	
4.10.p.m. do........	20th Battery fired 3 rounds at Germans in fire trench near point 51.	
5.p.m. do........	57th How Battery shelled U house point 252.	
5.20.p.m. do........	14th Battery fired at house R 16.	
6.30.p.m. do........	Batteries of R.A. Centre Group fired at enemy's infantry firing at our aeroplane.	
6.40.p.m. do........	Our aeroplane heavily fired on by E Section-2nd Battery fired on these trenches in reply.	
7.p.m. do........	Batteries of R.A. Centre Group fired 2 effective rounds at Germans (about 20 men) in S 11 b.	* Appendix 142.
	For further information see Tactical Progress Report. *	

Army Form C. 2118.

WAR DIARY
or
INTELLIGENCE SUMMARY.
(Erase heading not required.)

Instructions regarding War Diaries and Intelligence
Summaries are contained in F.S. Regs., Part II.
and the Staff Manual respectively. Title pages
will be prepared in manuscript.

Hour, Date, Place	Summary of Events and Information	Remarks and references to Appendices
3.30.a.m. 22nd April 1915. FOSSE	All batteries of R.A. Northern Group opened fire as ordered-firing 2 rounds per gun.	
8.a.m. do	30th How: Battery replied to enemy shelling our trenches and O.P. by shelling his trenches— hostile fire ceased.	
9.5.a.m. do	Batteries of R.A. Centre Group fired on party of men(observers) looking over trench S 11 b.	
11.a.m. do	Batteries of R.A. Centre Group fired on enemy's trenches from 128 to 131.	
11.15.a.m. do	Hostile aeroplane AVIATIK sighted, high, bearing 150°, engaged 4 rounds, turned E and was then out of range. 20th Battery fired 6 rounds at cross roads in N 25 b 3'3 where several germans were seen. 9th Battery fired few rounds at Chateau S 17 c 7'4 reported to be German Headquarters.	
11.30.a.m. do	19th Battery registered on their new zone on S 11 c and d.	
11.40.a.m. do	Batteries of R.A. Centre Group fired at house at point 65 reported as being O.P. 3 direct hits out of 8 rounds.	× appendix 154
11.45.a.m. do	Batteries of R.A. Centre Group fired at enemy's trenches from 63 to S 11 b 2'5.	
12.30.p.m. do	BAREILLY Brigade again asked for heavies to fire on point 204, apparently not being satisfied with damage done by 57th How: Battery at 2.10.p.m. yesterday.	
12.45.p.m. do	28th Battery registered points 46 and 49, and S 5 d 6'4.	
1.p.m. do	PORT ARTHUR shelled by 6 very heavy H.E.— probably Black Maria(8"How:).	
3.p.m. do	57th How: Battery shelled houses from point 202 to point 148, by request of "E" Section.	
3.15.p.m. do	20th Battery shelled sniper's house at haystack near point 260, as ordered to be done daily.	
4.p.m. do	Enemy heavy howitzer fired few rounds towards PORT ARTHUR.	
4.15.p.m. do	Hostile aeroplane AVIATIK, high, bearing 40°, engaged 26 rounds, turned S.E.	
4.35.p.m. do	57th How: Battery fired on houses in vicinity of point 204— the house pointed out by the Infantry was burnt to the ground and two more close by set alight.	
5.p.m. do	Enemy shelled RITZ corner.	

Army Form C. 2118.

WAR DIARY
or
INTELLIGENCE SUMMARY.
(Erase heading not required.)

Instructions regarding War Diaries and Intelligence Summaries are contained in F.S. Regs., Part II. and the Staff Manual respectively. Title pages will be prepared in manuscript.

Hour, Date, Place	Summary of Events and Information	Remarks and references to Appendices
5.10.p.m. 22nd April 1915. BOSSE.	German battery shelled our trenches in front of points XX 130 and 131.	+Appendix 1374
5.30 to 6.p.m. do........	10.5 cm. fired about 8 rounds close to 44th Battery position.	
5.55.p.m. do........	Hostile aeroplane, AVIATIK, high, bearing 150°, out of range, turned E.	
6.15.p.m. do........	Observing Officer 40th How:Battery observed flashes of German gun at N 26 c 6'5.	
6.40.p.m. do........	3.8" Howitzer shell fell near road at M 18 a 7'8.	*Appendix 2.143
7.p.m. do........	8" Howitzer shelled vicinity of M 10 c 1'1 from direction of HERLIES. *	Aug.
	For further information see Tactical Progress Report attached.	

Form/C. 2118/10
(9 29 6) W 4141—463 100,000 9/14 H W V

Army Form C. 2118.

WAR DIARY
or
INTELLIGENCE SUMMARY.
(Erase heading not required.)

Instructions regarding War Diaries and Intelligence Summaries are contained in F. S. Regs., Part II. and the Staff Manual respectively. Title pages will be prepared in manuscript.

Hour, Date, Place		Summary of Events and Information	Remarks and references to Appendices
6.a.m. 23rd April 1915. FOSSE.		8th Battery registered on trenches V6 to S 11 c 1'8 and 54 to S 11 c 9'6. A few rounds were fired at 3.45.p.m. at different points in these same trenches.	
6.15.a.m.	do	2nd Battery fired on enemy's wire and front trenches.	
9.a.m.	do	Enemy shelled house at M 38 d 8'2 from S.E. with light "hows."	
9.30.a.m.	do	Enemy 4'2 How made good practice on house at road junction M 32 d 5'4.	
10.48.a.m.	do	77 mm. fired a few rounds at 66th Battery O.P. and trenches in front of it. Batteries of R.A. Centre Group fired 2 rounds at enemy's O.P. at pt. 69 to stop PIPSQUEAK firing on our trenches.	× Appendix 134.
11.a.m.	do	German field howitzer shelled the MIN from the direction of AUBERS 6th West Riding F.A. Bde carried out registration on various points in "E" and "F" Sections. The 5th Battery West Riding Bde also registered on pts in "G" and "H" Sections. 2nd Battery registered on their new zone.	
1.30.p.m.	do	Operation Order No.16 by G.O.C., R.A., MEERUT Division issued.	* Appendix 144.
2.10.p.m.	do	PIPSQUEAK shelled vicinity M 27 b 8'2.	
2.15.p.m.	do	28th Battery registered on points 48, 68, and 18.	
2.45.p.m.	do	Enemy 4'2" How: shelled house in RUE du BOIS about 120 yards W, of RITZ hitting it once or twice.	
3.15.p.m.	do	Batteries of R.A. Centre Group fired a few rounds at movement in house at point 63. 14th Battery registered point 123.	
6.15.p.m.	do	About 12 rounds from 15 cm. batteryvfell round about 44th Battery, bearing of battery taken from M 31 d 6'8 was 131.	% Appendix 145.
=		For further information see Tactical Progress Report attached. N: 4 Indian Mortar Battery joined Meerut Divisional Artillery today	

Army Form C. 2118.

WAR DIARY
or
INTELLIGENCE SUMMARY.
(Erase heading not required.)

Instructions regarding War Diaries and Intelligence Summaries are contained in F.S. Regs., Part II. and the Staff Manual respectively. Title pages will be prepared in manuscript.

Hour, Date, Place	Summary of Events and Information	Remarks and references to Appendices
2.50.a.m. 24th April 1915. FOSSE.	Germans bombed Salient trench to which 2nd Battery replied.	
4.a.m. do	28th Battery fired 3 rounds on enemy's trenches in "H" Section.	
8.10.a.m. do	Hostile aeroplane sighted flying high, out of range, turned E. and returned to German lines.	
9 to 9.30.a.m. do	44th Battery fired a few rounds into German trenches who were firing at our aeroplane.	
11.40.a.m. do	German 6" How: fired 2 rounds near cross roads at M 15 c.	
11.30.a.m. do	8th Battery registered trench from 54× to S 11 c 9¹6.	
12.6.p.m. do	7th Battery fired a few rounds at point 129×	
12.50.p.m. do	14th Battery registered from point 140× to point 204×	
1.25 to 1.40.p.m. do	Enemy shelled over NEUVE CHAPELLE and 7th Battery Observation Post.	+appendix 154
1.45.p.m. do	19th Battery registered LIGNY le PETIT and trenches in S 11 d from their new position.	
3.30.p.m. do	At request of O.C. LONDON Regt 8th Battery fired few rounds at a M.G. emplacement at point 59.×	
3.45.p.m. do	Germans bombed our front trenches opposite "GOOD LUCK" House and PIPSQUEAK shelled CRESCENT Trench and RUE du BOIS.	
3.50.p.m. do	Germans bombed ORCHARD trench— bombing stopped by 2 rounds of lyddite from 30th How: Battery.	
	CRESCENT trench shelled from direction V 8 by PIPSQUEAK.	
4.p.m. do	14th Battery registered fire trench in front of point 66 and working party in communication trench.	
4 to 4.30.p.m. do	PORT ARTHUR and RUE du BOIS as far as S 9 d were shelled by German Howitzers and PIPSQUEAK.	
4.15.p.m. do	44th Battery fired in conjunction with heavies on V 8.	
4.30.p.m. do	57th How: Battery shelled point 204× by request of "E" Section— this point giving trouble from "bomb" guns every night.	
	For further information see Tactical Progress Report attached.	* Appendix 146.

Sn— to the withdrawal of the LAHORE Divison the relief— what of C.R.A MEERUT Divison Often Col. Gray No 16 was not carried out and the O.C. gul Bde R.F.A remained in command of the Meerut gp. in accordance with MEERUT Divison No I.G. 403/50/×.

2 Sections of the 30th How Bn/Bny were quartered with the R.A. Cable gp. for this purpose — see appendices 146(b)+(c).

M.R.9

×appendix 146(a)
×appendix 146(b)+146(c)

Army Form C. 2118.

WAR DIARY
or
INTELLIGENCE SUMMARY.
(Erase heading not required.)

Instructions regarding War Diaries and Intelligence Summaries are contained in F.S. Regs., Part II. and the Staff Manual respectively. Title pages will be prepared in manuscript.

Hour, Date, Place	Summary of Events and Information	Remarks and references to Appendices
11.a.m. 25th April 1915. FOSSE.	66th Battery fired at point 63.x	
11.30.a.m. do	20th Battery fired 6 rounds at houses near point 259.x	
11.45.a.m. do	7th Battery fired at party of men observed in communication trench near 65.	
12 noon do	5th Siege Battery registered houses 400 yards N.W. TOURELLE cross roads, points 50x and 51.x	x Appendix 154.
12 to 2.p.m. do	Enemy fired 10.5 c.m. into Brewery and neighbourhood from Ht POMMEREAU.	
3.p.m. do	8th Battery registered german trench between S 10 b 4·1 and S 10 b 9·4 - few rounds were also fired along the LA BASSEE Road near S 11 c 4·6.	
3.30.p.m. do	PIPSQUEAK shelled vicinity M 24 c 8·9 at long intervals. Observing Officer 66th Battery observed for 24th Heavy Battery along BOIS du BIEZ - 18 rounds were fired.	
3.35.p.m. do	19th Battery registered on "Machine Gun" House in M 36 d 7·8.	
3.35 to 4.p.m. do	19th Battery fired on above house with 10 H.E. obtaining 7 direct hits.	
4.p.m. do	Several German H.E. fired at 28th Battery O.P. M 23 d 3·3.	
4.15.p.m. do	14th Battery registered house M 36 d 2·7. PIPSQUEAK shelled area between the MIN and M 15 b.	
	*	* Appendix 147.
	For further information see Tactical Progress Report attached.	
	Orders received for MEERUT Divn. to W. & Lenal Mortar Battery to be placed at disposal of BAREILLY Bde for work tonight and tomorrow night - see appendix 147(a).	x Appendix 147(a).
	Grouping of MEERUT Divnl. Artillery after withdrawal of LAHORE Divn. is shown in appendix. 147(b).x	x Appendix 147(b).

Army Form C. 2118.

WAR DIARY
or
INTELLIGENCE SUMMARY.
(*Erase heading not required.*)

Instructions regarding War Diaries and Intelligence Summaries are contained in F.S. Regs., Part II. and the Staff Manual respectively. Title pages will be prepared in manuscript.

Hour, Date, Place		Summary of Events and Information	Remarks and references to Appendices
8.30.a.m. 26th April 1915. FOSSE.		20th Battery fired 2 rounds on German front trenches in "G" Section.	
11.a.m.	do........	8th Battery registered so as to concentrate fire on two points in trench at S.10 d 10·5 and S.10 d 6·5; also registered communication trench at V.6.(S.10 d 2·8) with object of catching enemy bringing up reliefs in the evening.	+ Appendix 157.
11.20.a.m.	do........	7th Battery fired on house 60 yards S.W. of 125—Infantry reported snipers active.	
11.30.a.m	do........	14th Battery fired on houses 123 and 124—Infantry cooperated with rifle fire.	
12.5.p.m.	do........	66th Battery fired on sandbag emplacement near 130.	
12.45.p.m.	do........	66th Battery fired on house 66 and on trenches in front of it.	
1.30.p.m.	do........	20th Battery fired 4 rounds on AUBERS Ridge.	
2.30.p.m.	do........	66th Battery fired on house at 69.	
3.p.m.	do........	PIPSQUEAK fired 15 rounds from N.E. of BOIS du BIEZ in vicinity of M.27 d—obtaining 4 direct hits on house at M 27 d 6·8.	
3.5.p.m.	do........	7th Battery fired at enemy O.P. point 85—3 hits on house.	
3.30.p.m.	do........	2nd Siege Battery registered on house on LA BASSEE Road S 11 c 2·8.	
3.40.p.m.	do........	66th Battery fired on barricade at point 133.	
4.p.m.	do........	20th Battery fired 4 rounds on machine gun emplacement at MIN du PIETRE.	
5.30.p.m.	do........	PIPSQUEAK shelled house near cross roads at M 34 b 5·7.	
6.15 to 7.p.m.	do........	Enemy shelled 66th Battery O.P. and NEUVE CHAPELLE with heavy howitzer	
		66th Battery responded by firing on German trenches.	
6.20.p.m.	do........	7th Battery fired on German trenches to stop rifle fire at our aeroplane which was flying very low.	
6.45.p.m.	do........	2 heavy bombs fell at M 29 c 6·6 and "F" Section was heavily bombed at the same time from point 204. 19th Battery opened fire on this point and bombing ceased.	
6.48.p.m.	do........	Enemy shelled NEUVE CHAPELLE and our support trenches at M 29 c 2·6.	
		Our Infantry bombed points 202 and 203.	
7.p.m.	do........	Enemy shelled locality of our "bomb" gun opposite point 202 and road at M 35 a 7·5.	
		For further information see Tactical Progress Report attached.	* Appendix 148.

Army Form C. 2118.

WAR DIARY
or
INTELLIGENCE SUMMARY.
(Erase heading not required.)

Instructions regarding War Diaries and Intelligence Summaries are contained in F.S. Regs., Part II. and the Staff Manual respectively. Title pages will be prepared in manuscript.

Hour, Date, Place	Summary of Events and Information	Remarks and references to Appendices
7.15.p.m. 26th April 1915. FOSSE.	Enemy bombed our trenches from point 204–19th Battery replied on this point and bombing ceased. Forward Observing Officer 28th Battery at the MIN (M 22 d 2'5) reported 2 flashes seen–true bearings 117°30' and 115°30'. 20th Battery from MOATED GRANGE (M 29) reported flashes–true bearings 116°30' and 111°30'–guns thought to be behind a hedge.	× Appendix 174.
7.40.p.m. do	Enemy bombed SALIENT trench and the 2nd Battery replied on point 204 and it ceased.	
9.45.p.m. do	Forward Observing Officer 28th Battery reported exceptionally heavy traffic in direction of AUBERS.	M29.
10.20.p.m. do	BAREILLY Brigade reported 4 light field guns located in wood behind point 206, and that enemy were cutting down trees, possibly to clear field of fire.	×Appendix 148(a).
10.30.p.m. do	19th Battery fired on working party cutting down trees near point 206– this was repeated at 11.30.a.m.	
12 midnight do	28th Battery fired 6 rounds on points 257 and 263 as requested by the Infantry.	
12.15.a.m. 27th April 1915. FOSSE.	19th Battery opened searching fire for guns located in wood behind point×206. MEERUT Division Operation Order No. 28 received.	
1.a.m. do	28th Battery again fired 6 rounds at 257×and 263.×	
11.a.m. do	2nd Battery registered on machine gun emplacement 20 yards N.E. of 140.	
12.10.p.m. do	66th Battery registered point 52.×	
12.15.p.m. do	Enemy fired 5 bombs at "listening post" from rear of trench of point 140– 2nd Battery replied.	
12.30.p.m. do	14th Battery fired 2 rounds at house 100 yards S. of 151.	
1.p.m. do	3 shell fell near road junction M 26.a.	
1.10.p.m. do	PIPSQUEAK shelled our trenches in "E" Sub-section. Enemy again bombed from near point 140 at our "listening post" and house in M 35 d 4'7–2nd Battery replied obtaining direct hits on parapet.	
1.15.p.m. do	4'2 How: shelled NEUVE CHAPELLE from direction N 31.a. Enemy's field gun fired 6 rounds on point M 34 b 3'4 from S.E. direction.	
1.20.p.m. do	5'9" How: shelled ROUGE CROIX and vicinity M 22 c from direction HAUTE POMMEREAU.	
1.50.p.m. do	Enemy's 4" gun fired on rese ve trenches in rear of NEUVE CHAPELLE.	

Army Form C. 2118.

WAR DIARY
or
INTELLIGENCE SUMMARY.
(Erase heading not required.)

Instructions regarding War Diaries and Intelligence Summaries are contained in F.S. Regs., Part II. and the Staff Manual respectively. Title pages will be prepared in manuscript.

Hour, Date, Place	Summary of Events and Information	Remarks and references to Appendices
27th April 1915. FOSSE.	German field howitzer flashes observed, magnetic bearing from MIN (M 22 d 2'4) 141°.	*Appendix 154
2.20.p.m. do.	Same battery's flashes observed from house M 23 d 3'5-143°30'.	
2.35.p.m. do.	Heavy fire heard from FAUQUISSART and reported as chiefly shrapnel.	
3.p.m. do.	14th Battery fired at house at cross roads near point 125.*	
4.p.m. do.	7th Battery fired a few rounds at snipers in German trenches.	
4.20.p.m. do.	30th How: Battery registered trenches at Points 137* and 128.*	* Appendix 150
4.30.p.m. do.	66th Battery fired at point 69.*	
5.45.p.m. do.	Operation Order No.17 by C.O.,R.A. issued. *	* Appendix 149.
3.30.p.m. do.	For further information see Tactical Progress Report attached.	MR9 + appendix 150
	One section of the 19th and 20th Batteries moved to new positions at M 26 d 4.4 and M 33 a 3.7 respectively in accordance with C.R.A Operation Order N°17.	

Forms/C. 2118/10

WAR DIARY
or
INTELLIGENCE SUMMARY.
(Erase heading not required.)

Army Form C. 2118.

Hour, Date, Place	Summary of Events and Information	Remarks and references to Appendices
8.40.a.m. 28th April 1915. FOSSE.	Enemy shelled suppt trenches behind NEUVE CHAPELLE with H.E. and shrapnel from direction of HAUTE POMMEREAU.	
8.42.a.m. do	Enemy shelled NEUVE CHAPELLE with guns and PIPSQUEAK.	
8.45.a.m. do	Batteries of the Centre Group shelled German trench near point 140 in retaliation to German shelling NEUVE CHAPELLE.	
8.45.a.m. do	Hostile aeroplane AVIATIK sighted flying high, bearing 115°, engaged 8 rounds by ARCHIBALD and turned S.E.	
9.30.a.m. do	PIPSQUEAK active on Gurkha Headquarters from N.E. edge of BOIS du BIEZ— this was repeated at 11.a.m., 11.15.a.m. and 12.30.p.m.	
9.55.a.m. do	PIPSQUEAK fired 2 rounds on "E" Sub-section support trenches from direction AUBERS.	
10.a.m. do	Section of 30th How: Battery fired at point 130.	
10.15.a.m. do	Hostile aeroplane AVIATIK sighted high, bearing 115°, engaged 43 rounds, turned E. and disappeared. Re-appeared and again engaged with 27 rounds, turned N.N.E. out of range.	+ appendix 15+
10.20.a.m. do	German field howitzer shelled vicinity of M 23 d 4'3.	
10.25.a.m. 25 do	Same battery(probably) shelled road junction at M 22 c 3'5 from direction of HAUTE POMMEREAU.	
10.30.a.m. do	Hostile aeroplane FOKKER seen high, bearing 75°, engaged 2 rounds, turned E, out of range.	
10.45.a.m. do	66th Battery fired on point 130.	
11.a.m. do	Our trench mortar fired 4 rounds from S 35 d 3'5 on enemy's trench S 36 c 3'7.	
11.20.a.m. do	66th Battery fired on trench at L in BRULOT.	
11.25.a.m. do	Enemy bombed "Swan Neck" trench M 36 a. in reply.	
11.30.a.m. do	28th Battery fired 4 rounds Fremxs at Sniper's House (263) and 3 rounds at point 260 by request of Infantry.	
11.50.a.m. do	2nd Battery fired 4 rounds at N.W. corner of BOIS du BIEZ.	12.5p. Orders recd for 1st battery for all live pipes on protruding over enemy trenches to be destroyed by Artillery fire forthwith vide message No G41/4 from 1st MEERUT Division. + Appendix 15/(2)
1.30.p.m. do	German 4'2 How fired one round at M 35 c 4'9.	
2.p.m. do	German 4'2 How fired few rounds at house M 32 d 8'2.	
2.15.p.m. do	Enemy 4'2 shelled O.P. of 5th Siege Battery S 3 c 5'8.	
2.30.p.m. do	German battery shelled house in vicinity of M 22 c 3'9.	
2.45.p.m. to 3.5.p.m. do	28th Battery fired on "hose pipe" visible about 50 yards E. of point 257, with H.E. and shrapnel—3 direct hits were obtained with shrapnel just to one side and 2 rounds last.	

P.T.O.

Army Form C. 2118.

WAR DIARY
or
INTELLIGENCE SUMMARY.
(Erase heading not required.)

Instructions regarding War Diaries and Intelligence Summaries are contained in F.S. Regs., Part II. and the Staff Manual respectively. Title pages will be prepared in manuscript.

Hour, Date, Place	Summary of Events and Information	Remarks and references to Appendices
3.p.m. 28th April 1915. FOSSE.	destroyed a large piece of the enemy's parapet just in rear-sand-bags flew in all directions and hose pipe disappeared. 8th Battery engaged hose pipe in S 10 b 5'4-fired 9 shrapnel and 3 H.E. 5 direct hits on parapet, one H.E. detonated just behind the parapet throwing up a large column of water- considerable damage was done to parapet.	× appendix 154.
4.p.m. do.	German field battery replied on our trenches.	
4.30.p.m. do.	Same battery fired several rounds of gun fire on CHAPIGNY followed by field howitzer fire.	
5.p.m. do.	PIPSQUEAK shelled house at M 35 c 8'7.	
6.5.p.m. do.	PIPSQUEAK again fired one round at M 35 c 8'7.	
6.15.p.m. do.	66th Battery fired on hose pipe at point 131 and destroyed it.×	
	7th Battery fired 16 rounds on the two hose pipes near point 166, direct hits obtained on the parapet at both points.	
6.40.p.m. do.	Enemy howitzer shelled PORT ARTHUR.	
8.45.p.m. do.	44th Battery fired 25 rounds on hose pipe near point 57-several rounds hit parapet close by.	
7.15 to 7.45.p.m. do.	Several PIPSQUEAK shell fell about 7 R 34 b 3'5, all were blind except two which burst in the air.	* Appendix 151.
	*	
	For further information see Tactical Progress Report attached.	WWSS

Army Form C. 2118.

WAR DIARY
or
INTELLIGENCE SUMMARY.
(Erase heading not required.)

Instructions regarding War Diaries and Intelligence Summaries are contained in F.S. Regs., Part II. and the Staff Manual respectively. Title pages will be prepared in manuscript.

Hour, Date, Place	Summary of Events and Information	Remarks and references to Appendices
4.30.a.m. 29th April 1915. FOSSE.	8th Battery fired on German trench in front of ORCHARD Redoubt at request of Infantry in order to stop bombing with desired effect.	
7 to 7.20.a.m. do.	Enemy 4'2" How: fired about 30 rounds at house at cross roads M 35 & 8'3-obtaining 3 direct hits.	
7.15 to 7.40.p.m. do.	PORT ARTHUR shelled by 5'9" and again at 2.30.p.m.	
7.20.a.m. do.	Enemy shelled our support trenches of "F" Sub-section with H.E. and shrapnel from direction of HAUTE POMMEREAU.	
8.10.a.m. do.	Hostile aeroplane ALBATROSS sighted flying high, bearing 80°, out of range, turned S.E. over German lines.	
9.12.a.m. do.	Hostile aeroplane AVIATIK flying high, bearing 60°, engaged with 78 rounds, turned E.N.E. over German lines, reappeared at bearing 45° engaged with 38 rounds, turned E. over German lines out of range.	*appendix 153*
10.50.a.m. do.	4'2" shelled house at cross roads M 35 & 8'3 from direction HAUTE POMMEREAU.	
11.15.a.m. do.	66th Battery fired a few rounds on houses near 63 and 65—the latter was set on fire.	
11.55.a.m. do.	7th Battery fired on house 63 reported by Infantry to contain machine gun. 44th Battery fired on working party at 55.	
12.30.p.m. do.	8th Battery registered a point near V.6. from which hostile bombing takes place.	
1 to 1.25.p.m. do.	PIPSQUEAK shelled vicinity of 44th Battery O.P.	
1.30.p.m. do.	PIPSQUEAK shelled GOOD LUCK House.	
2.p.m. do.	3 rounds 5'9" How fell near PORT ARTHUR.	
3.30.p.m. do.	PIPSQUEAK fired on party proceeding along road running through M 28 b and M 22 c.	
3.45.p.m. do.	PIPSQUEAK fired on reserve trenches in M 28 b.	
4.20.p.m. do.	PIPSQUEAK did good shooting at haystack in front of MIN at M 22 d 2'2 and then turned on to PONT du HEM.	
4.30.p.m. do.	14th Battery fired on house 100 yards S.W. of 151 with haystack and evidently dug-out on its right.	
4.45.p.m. do.	66th Battery fired 8 rounds at snipers in house near 65.	
5.15.p.m. do.	Section of 30th How: Battery registered road junction 125.	

For further information see Tactical Progress Report attached.

*Appendix 152.

Army Form C. 2118.

WAR DIARY
or
INTELLIGENCE SUMMARY.
(Erase heading not required.)

Instructions regarding War Diaries and Intelligence Summaries are contained in F.S. Regs., Part II. and the Staff Manual respectively. Title pages will be prepared in manuscript.

Hour, Date, Place	Summary of Events and Information	Remarks and references to Appendices
9.10.a.m. 30th April 1915.	8th Battery fired 2 shrapnel at machine gun at point 50 at request of O.C. 6th Jats.	
10.5.a.m.	66th Battery fired at house 65.	
11.25.a.m.	7th Battery fired a few rounds at snipers near point 131 reported by Infantry.	
11.35.a.m.	Hostile aeroplane AVIATIK sighted flying high between 11,000 and 12,000 feet, appear from N.N.E. and travelled W. Identification marks black cross on white disc, giving appearance of rings at a distance. Engaged with 18 rounds, plane dropped suddenly after first round and then went on in a Westerly direction. See also Tactical Progress Report*.	* Appendix 153.
11.40.a.m.	German heavy howitzer shelled 7th Battery O.P. from AUBERS Ridge.	
11.55.a.m.	66th Battery fired at enemy O.P. at 65.	
12.15.a.m.	66th Battery fired on "L" shaped house, men pt 125.	× appendix 164.
12.20.p.m.	German aeroplane dropped a bomb 800 yards S. of the MEERUT Division Ammunition Column wounding 2 women.	
3.p.m.	8th Battery again fired on machine gun at 59-firing 6 shrapnel and 7 H.E.-fire effective breaking up parapet where machine gun located.	
3.30.p.m.	PORT ARTHUR shelled with 5'9 Howitzers from direction of ILLIES, also shelled at 4.45.p.m. PIPSQUEAK also shelled same place at the same time.	
4.p.m.	PIPSQUEAK shelled the RUE du BOIS.	
4.6.p.m.	PIPSQUEAK had 8 direct hits on 7th Battery O.P.	
4.10.p.m. and 4.50 to 5.15.p.m.	German 10'5 c.m. fired about 15 rounds which fell close to PORT ARTHUR.	
6.p.m.	14th Battery fired on trenches at 145 and 66th fired at trenches at 130 to 13½ to keep down rifle fire on our aeroplane.	
6.5p.m.	2nd Siege Battery registered LORGIES with aeroplane-fired 2 rounds percussion shrapnel—both unobserved—then fired a round of lyddite which was given as target.	
6.50.p.m.	14th Battery fired on likely observing house at M 36 d 5'5.	
	For further information see tactical progress report attached. N° 4 Trench Mortar Battery proceeded at noon to the ORCHARD	* Appendix 153. × Appendix 153(a)

Army Form C. 2118.

WAR DIARY
or
INTELLIGENCE SUMMARY.
(*Erase heading not required.*)

Instructions regarding War Diaries and Intelligence Summaries are contained in F.S. Regs., Part II. and the Staff Manual respectively. Title pages will be prepared in manuscript.

Hour, Date, Place	Summary of Events and Information	Remarks and references to Appendices
	* A map showing the sections of the Indian Corps front is attached.	* Appendix 154(a)
1st May 1915	[signed] M. Reynolds Saunders Major R.A. Brigade Major, Royal Artillery, MEERUT DIVISION.	

"A" Form.   Army Form C. 2121.
MESSAGES AND SIGNALS.   No. of Message _____

SECRET

APPENDIX 130

TO: C.R.A.

Sender's Number: QC577   Day of Month: 2nd   AAA

9th and 13th Bdes R.F.A. and 43rd (How.) Bde rejoin Meerut Division probably tomorrow aaa You will arrange to meet them and direct the two formations to billets in the triangle ST VENANT (exclusive) ROBECQ, BUSNES (inclusive) aaa the one By. of 43rd Bde will, it is in-

"A" Form.
Army Form C. 2121.

MESSAGES AND SIGNALS.   No. of Message_____

| Prefix____ Code____ m. | Words. | Charge. | This message is on a/c of: | Recd. at____ m. |
| Office of Origin and Service Instructions. | Sent At____ m. To____ By____ | | ____Service. (Signature of "Franking Officer.") | Date____ From____ By____ |

TO {

| Sender's Number | Day of Month | In reply to Number | A A A |

tended, go into action aaa the other Battery and Bde. H.Q. will be billeted near the 30th Bay. if possible or failing this in the above mentioned Triangle. aaa definite orders re march will issue later

From   Meerut Division
Place
Time   B J H_____
The above may be forwarded as now corrected. (Z)

Censor.   Signature of Addressor or person authorised to telegraph in his name
* This line should be erased if not required.

"A" Form. Army Form C. 2121.
MESSAGES AND SIGNALS. APPENDIX 131

TO — C R A Meerut Divn.

Sender's Number: G370/2　Day of Month: 2nd　In reply to Number: —　AAA

Following wire received from Indian Corps begins

Direct 9th and 13th Brigades R.F.A. to march to CALONNE during night 3rd/4th April AAA Route road junction square M/21/A Cross Roads R/28/D Fosse L'EPINETTE GRAND PACAUT AAA Please inform Meerut Division direct hour at which leading Brigade will reach CALONNE AAA Meerut Division will arrange meet these Brigades and direct them to billeting areas. Addressed 7th Divn. repeated Meerut and Lahore Divisions and 4th Corps ends

For information and necessary action

P. Davies
Major.
General Staff, Meerut Division

APPENDIX 132

Copy of a memo No.G-483, dated 2nd April 1915,
Received from Indian Corps.

In continuation of G-464 of 2nd April 1915, and in substitution of G-467 of 2nd April 1915, following is detail of moves referred to therein :-

1. **9th Brigade R.F.A.** rejoin the Indian Corps night 3rd/4th April, and billets in Area St. Venant (exclusive) - BUSNES - ROBECQ.
   Starting point - Road junction K.35.d.5.8.
   Time 8.30 p.m.
   Route - LE GRAND PACAUT - LE PETIT PACAUT - CALONNE.
   Section D.A.C. 9th Brigade R.F.A. rejoins Meerut D.A.C. at ROBECQ on morning 4th April via St. Venant.
   Proportion of Park. rejoins No.1 Indian Ammunition Park at St. Venant morning 4th April.

2. **13th Brigade R.F.A.** Rejoins Indian Corps night 4/5th April and billets in area ST. VENANT (exclusive)- BUSNES - ROBECQ.
   Starting point - Cross Roads R.5.a.
   Time 9.0 pm.
   ROUTE - LESTREM - L'EPINETTE - road junction Q.12.c. - GRAND PACAUT - CALONNE.
   Section D.A.C. Proportion of Park) as in 1 above but on morning of 5th April.

3. **43rd (How) Bde. (Less 30th Batty.)** 40th Battery to relieve 35th Battery (37th Brigade) in square M.32.b.3.9.on night 4/5th April.
   Bde. H.Q. and 57th Battery to billets in Area ST. VENANT (exclusive) - BUSNES - ROBECQ.
   Starting point - LAVENTIE.
   Time - 8.0 p.m.
   Route - M'AU MONDE, ESTAIRES- MERVILLE-CALONNE
   Section D.A.C. 43rd(How) Bde. Rejoins Lahore D.A.C. at CALONNE on morning 5th April, via GRAND PACAUT.
   Proportion of Park. Rejoins No.1 Indian Ammunition Park at St. Venant morning 5th April.

4. Orders for the above moves are being given by G.O.C., 7th Divn.

5. Meerut Division will arrange for the 9th, 13th and 43rd Bdes. being met on arrival at CALONNE and conducted to billeting areas.

6. On relief by 40th(How) Battery on night 4/5th April, 35th (How) Battery to rejoin 7th Division under orders to be given by G.O.C. Lahore Division in communication with G.O.C. 7th Division.

7. 5th Siege Battery to remain in it's present position and to come under orders of G.O.C. 7th Division at 6.0 a.m. 5th April 1915.

No.G-370/3.   3rd April 1915.

Memorandum,
   For information and necessary action.

   Major.
   General Staff, Meerut Division.

To,
   C.R.A.

APPENDIX 133.

OPERATION ORDER No 26
by
Lieutenant General Sir Charles ANDERSON, K.C.B.,
Commanding MEERUT Division.

Copy No............

Reference map FRANCE 1/40000.
Sheets 36 and 36A.

9th April 1915.

INFORMATION.	1. The Indian Corps in addition to the front now held is taking over a portion of the front now held by the 1st Division, up to and including the ORCHARD about 400 yards S.W. of PORT ARTHUR.
INTENTION.	2. The Meerut Division will relieve the Lahore Division (less Sappers and Pioneers), and units of the 1st Division now holding the new portion of front which is to be taken over on the nights 11th/12th and 12th/13th April.
RELIEFS. Bareilly Brigade.	3. (a) Bareilly Brigade will take over the line held by the Ferozepore Brigade on the night 11th/12th and that held by Jullunder Brigade on the night 12th/13th April. Headquarters M.14.b.10.0. Brigade Reserve billets - Rugby Road.
Dehra Dun Bde.	(b) Dehra Dun Brigade will take over from the 2nd Infantry Brigade the line East of LA BASSEE - ESTAIRE Road (road exclusive) on the nights 11th/12th and 12th/13th April. Headquarters M.33.a.1.6. Brigade Reserve billets - RUE DU PUITS and in that portion of road in M 33 a and b
Garhwal Brigade.	(c) Garhwal Brigade will take over with one and half battalion the line from 2nd and 1st Infantry Brigades from LA BASSEE - ESTAIRE Road inclusive to ORCHARD inclusive on night 12th/13th April. Headquarters LA COUTURE. Brigade Reserve. half battalion at Al work. Remainder of Brigade (2½ Bns) will be in Divisional Reserve.
Details of Reliefs.	(d) All details connected with the above reliefs will be arranged mutually by Brigade Command as concerned. Brigade Commanders will assume command of the line as reliefs are completed, reporting the same to Divisional Headquarters at once.
Movements.	(e) Movements will be carried out as in the attached March Table.
ARTILLERY.	4. Meerut Divisional Artillery including 43rd Howitzer Brigade relieve that of Lahore and 1st Divisions on nights 13th/14th and 14th/15th April under arrangements to be made mutually by G.O's.C. R.A., 1st, Lahore and Meerut Divisions
4th INDIAN CAVALRY.	5. 4th Indian Cavalry will exchange billets with 15th Indian Lancers on the afternoon 10th April. Time and route to be so arranged as not to interfere with moves of Garhwal and Sirhind Brigades.
SAPPERS & MINERS AND PIONEERS.	6. Nos 3 and 4 Companies, Sappers and Miners and 107th Indian Pioneers will remain in their present billets. Sappers and Miners and Pioneers Lahore Division are remaining in their present billets and will continue to be employed in the front area.
AMMUNITION SUPPLY.	7. Lahore Divisional Ammunition Column will continue to supply Ammunition.
MEDICAL.	8. Reliefs of Field Ambulances will take place partly on afternoon 10th April. Remainder of movements will be completed on 13th April. Arrangements for them will be made mutually between A.D.M.S., 1st, Lahore and Meerut Divisions.

(2).

REFILLING POINT. 9. Brigades will exchange Refilling Points on the days following exchange of billets. Refilling on the 10th April will be as at present. Details of refilling on 11th, 12th and 13th April will be issued separately.

TRAIN. 10. Companies of Meerut Divisional Train, except Divisional Troops Company, will exchange billets on the same days and the same routes as their Brigades. Supply Sections after refilling and Headquarters of Train Coys following Brigades.

COMMANDS. 11. G.O.C. Meerut Division will take over command of the lin from G.O.C's. 1st and Lahore Divisions at 8-.a.m. on 13th April.
Divisional Headquarters unaltered.

C. Norie.
Colonel.
General Staff,
MEERUT DIVISION.

Issued at 1.p.m. to
Signal Company.

Copy No 1. Indian Corps.
" " 2. Lahore Division.
" " 3. 1st Division.
" " 4. Dehra Dun Brigade.
" " 5 Garhwal Brigade.
" " 6. Bareilly Brigade.
" " 7. C.R.A. Meerut Division
" " 8. C.R.E. Meerut Division.
" " 9. 4th Indian Cavalry.
" " 10. 107th Indian Pioneers.
" " 11. Meerut Signal Company.

Copy No 12. Meerut Divisional Train.
" " 13. A.D.M.S. Meerut.
" " 14. A.A. Q.M.G.
" " 15. D.A.A.G.
" " 16. D.A.A. & Q.M.G.
" " 17.)
" " 18.) War diary
" " 19.)   &
" " 20.) Files.
" " 21.)

MARCH TABLE. (To accompany MEERUT Div. O.O. 26)

Date.	Brigade.	From.	To.	Route.	Remarks.
April 10th.	GARHWAL Bde.	Area No 6.	Area No 3.	CLARENCE ROAD, RUES DES VACHES, LE CORNET MALO, LESLOBES, VIEILLE CHAPELLE.	Units to be billeted E. of LESTREM-LOCON Rd not to cross it between 9.a.m and 12 noon. Head of column to pass ZELOBES at 11.a.m
	Sirhind Bde.	Area No 7.	Area No 6.	LOCON-LESTREM Road, LESTREM, L'EPINETTE, GD PACAUT.	
April 11th & night 11th/12th.	BAREILLY Bde.	Are No 5.	2 Bns to trenches in Southern Section in relief of Ferozepore Bde. Remainder of Bde to Area No 2.	ZELOBES, VIEILLE CHAPEL E, BOUT DEVILLE, PONT DU HEM.	LESTREM-LOCON Rd not to be crossed between 9.a.m. & 12 noon. No movement east of BOUT DEVILLE before 6.p.m. 2 battalions of Dehra Dun Bde to march under orders of Bareilly Bde, and to follow its leading two battalions from BOUT DEVILLE
	2 Battalions DEHRA DUN Bde.	Area No 4.	Portion of 1st Divn trenches east of LA BASSEE Road.	CIX MARMEUSE, ZELOBES, VIEILLE CHAPELLE, BOUT DEVILLE, PONT DU HEM.	
	Ferozepore Bde	Trenches Southern Section and Area No 2.	Area No 5.	Road Junction M.27.d., CIX BARBEE Road Junction M.2C.c. VIEILLE CHAPELLE, ZELOBES.	
April 12th & night 12th/13th.	DEHRA DUN Bde. (less 2 Bns.)	Area No 4.	Remainder of 1st Divn. trenches E. of LA BASSEE Road, and in Reserve.	CIX MARMEUSE, FOSSE, BOUT DEVILLE, CROIX BARBEE, Road Junction M.27.d.	LESTREM-LOCON Road not to be crossed between 9.am and 12 noon. No movement East of BOUT DEVILLE before 6.p.m. X Westward traffic over FOSSE Bridge to be held up by Lahore Division during passage of DEHRA DUN Brigade.

(2)

Date.	Brigade.	From.	To.	Route.	Remarks.
April 12th & night 12th/13th.	BAIEILLY Bde. (less 2 battns)	Area No 2.	Trenches in Northern Section and in Reserve, in relief of Jullunder Bde.		
	Jullunder Bde.	Trenches North-ern Section & Area No 1.	Area No 4.	ROUGE CROIX, PONT DU HEM, PIT MARAIS, PONT RIQUEL, LESTREM.	
	Garhwal Bde.	Area No 3.	VIEILLE CHAPELLE and LA COUTURE.	LESLOBES, ZELOBES, VIEILLE CHAPELLE Road Junction R.35.a.	
			1 battalion Garhwal Bde to trenches on RUE DU BOIS.	Route for this battalion will be notified later.	

In above table the billeting area now occupied by Jullunder Brigade is referred to as Area No 1.
                Ferozepore Brigade.   No 2.
                Sirhind Brigade.   No 3.
                Dehra Dun Brigade.   No 4.
                Bareilly Brigade.   No 5.
                Garhwal Brigade   No 6.

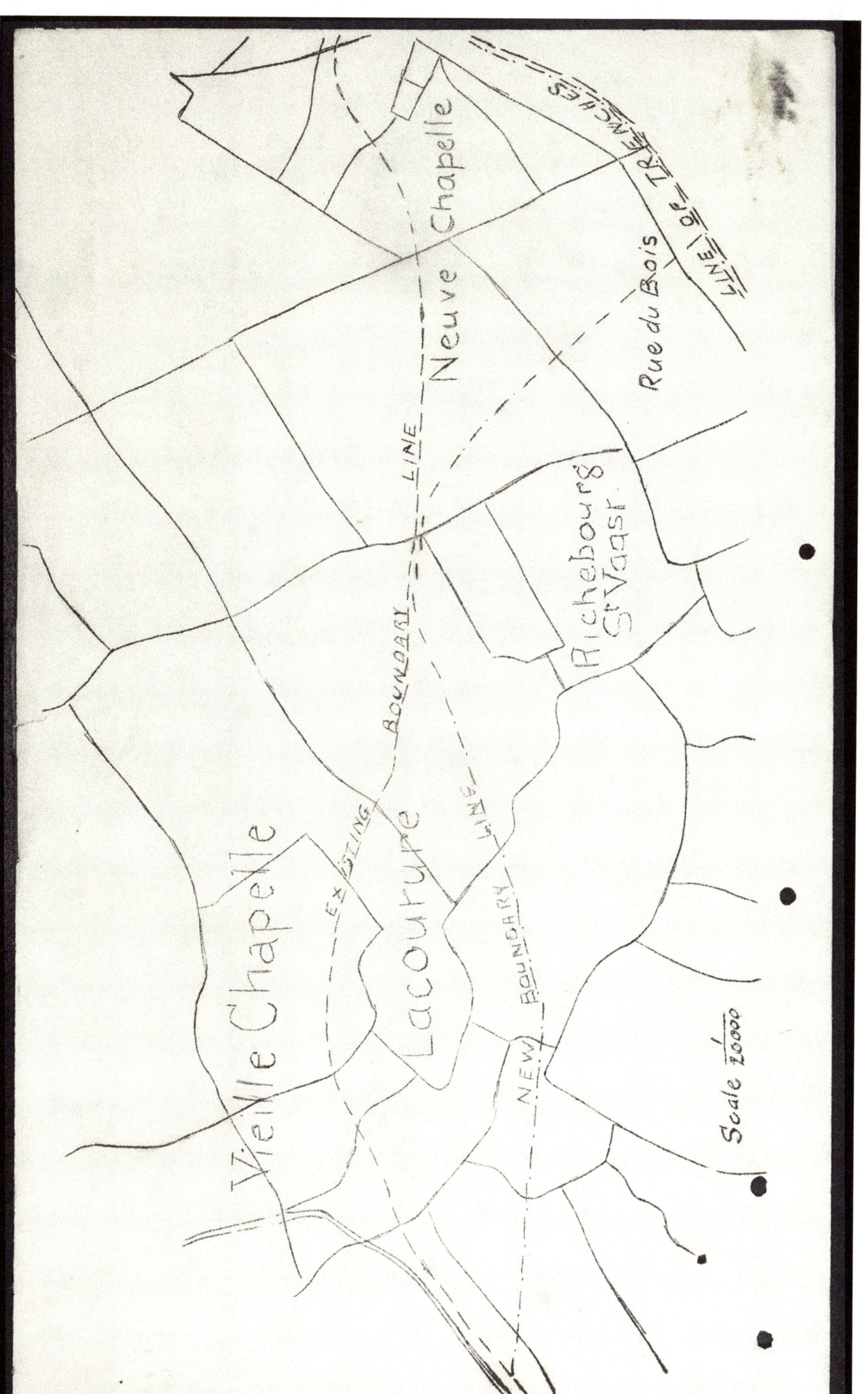

Copy No. 13
10th. April 1915.
OPERATION ORDER No. 15. APPENDIX 134

Brigadier General R.St.G.LECKY
Commanding Royal Artillery, MEERUT Division.

REFERENCE map FRANCE 1/40000.
Sheets 36 and 36A.

INFORMATION. 1. The Indian Corps in addition to the front now held is taking over a portion of the front now held by the 1st. Division, up to and including the ORCHARD about 400 yards S.W. of PORT ARTHUR.

INTENTION. 2. The MEERUT Divisional Artillery with 43rd. Howitzer Brigade R.F.A. and 2nd. Siege Battery R.G.A. will relieve the artillery of the LAHORE and 1st. Divisions between 11th. and 15th. of April.

GROUPS. 3. (a) Northern Group R.A. 9th. Brigade R.F.A.
O.C. Lt. Col. Potts R.F.A. 2nd. Battery R.F.A.
57th (How) Battery R.F.A.
will be grouped with BAREILLY Brigade which will hold the entire front at present held by the LAHORE Division.
Headquarters BAREILLY Brigade will be at M 14 b 10.0.

(b) Centre Group R.A. 4th. Brigade R.F.A.
O.C.Col.L.A.C.GORDON R.F.A. 44th. Battery R.F.A.
40th. (How) Batty.R.F.A.
will be grouped with DEHRA DUN Brigade which will hold the front from the Southern end of the line at present held by the LAHORE Division to LA BASSEE road exclusive.
Headquarters DEHRA DUN Brigade will be at M.31 d.5.7.

(c) Southern Group R.A. 8th. Battery R.F.A.
O.C.Lt.Col.L.A.TYLER R.F.A. 30th.(How) Batty.R.F.A.
will be grouped with the GARHWAL Brigade which will hold the front from the LA BASSEE road to the ORCHARD in S 10 b both inclusive.
Headquarters GARHWAL Brigade will be at LA COUTURE X 5 a.

Reference (a) LAHORE Divisional Artillery will be responsible for the artillery defence of this front till 12 noon 15th. instant.
Reference (b) and (c) 1st. Divisional Artillery will be responsible for the artillery defence of these two groups till 12 noon 15th. instant.

2nd. SIEGE BATTY. 4. 2nd. Siege Battery will be at the disposal of the G.O.C., R.A.

RELIEFS. 5. Artillery reliefs will be carried out in accordance with the attached MARCH TABLE.

AMMUNITION SUPPLY. 6. The Brigade Ammunition Columns will supply S.A.A. to the Infantry Brigades with which they are grouped and 18 Pr. ammunition to all 18 Pr. batteries in their Group Officers commanding 4th., 9th. and 13th. Brigades R.F.A. will establish the S.A.A. Sections of their Brigade Ammunition Columns in sufficient time to take up the supply of S.A.A. to the Infantry Brigades with which they are grouped. Instructions of Infantry Brigades should be requested on this point.
The LAHORE Divisional Ammunition Column will continue the supply of ammunition. LAHORE Divisional Ammunition Column is at CALONNE.

COMMUNICATIONS. 7. Attention is invited to Circular memo' No. 403 R.A.(L) dated 10-4-15 which has been issued to all concerned.

COMMANDS.   8.   G. O. C., R. A. MEERUT Division will assume command of the Artillery from G. O. C., R. A. 1st. and LAHORE Divisions from 12 noon 15th. instant.
Position of MEERUT Divisional Artillery Headquarters will remain unchanged.

R. V. Lynch-Staunton

Major R. A.,
Brigade Major Royal Artillery,
MEERUT DIVISION.

Issued at 8 p.m.
by Mounted Orderly.

Copy No. 1 to General Staff, MEERUT Divn.
Copy No. 2 to G.O.C., R.A. LAHORE Division.
Copy No. 3 to G.O.C., R.A. 1st. Division.
Copy No. 4 to G.O.C., DEHRA DUN Brigade.
Copy No. 5 to G.O.C., GARHWAL Brigade.
Copy No. 6 to G.O.C., BAREILLY Brigade.
Copy No. 7 to O.C. 4th. Brigade R.F.A.
Copy No. 8 to O.C. 8th. Brigade R.F.A.
Copy No. 9 to O.C. 13th. Brigade R.F.A.
Copy No.10 to O.C. 43rd. Brigade R.F.A.
Copy No.11 to O.C. 2nd. Siege Battery R.G.A.
Copy No.12 to O.C. MEERUT Divisional Ammn. Column.
Copy No.13 to War Diary.
Copy No.14 to FILE.

MARCH TABLE

DATE	UNIT	FROM	TO	TIME	ROUTE	REMARKS
13th	368th Bty R.F.A.	BUSNES	ETON RD. PONT du HEM	6.30 p.m.	ROBECQ, CALONNE, PONT RIQUEL & LCB O. to OXFORD RD. ETON RD.	To take up position in N sec. & sect. on 11-6-15. To arrive after 8.30 p.m.
13th	1 Section 71st Bty. R.F.A.	RIEZ du VINAGE	CROIX BARBET	6.30 p.m.	CORNET MALO CTS LA CREUSE FOSSE MARLBOROUGH RD. OXFORD RD.	To relieve one Section 64th Battery. To arrive after 8.30 p.m.
12th	1 Section 104th Bty. R.F.A.	LA BRASSERIE	do	6.30 p.m.	ROBECQ ST, VENISSE ON CORNET MALO CR. MARLBOROUGH RD.	To relieve one Section 81st Battery
12th	1 Sect 8th Battery	LA BRASSERIE	do	do	do	
13th	366th Bty R.F.A.	BUSNES	RUGBY ROAD	6.30 p.m.	ROBECQ CALONNE LESTREM PONT RIQUEL OXFORD RD and ETON RD.	To relieve 34th Bty. To arrive after 8.30 p.m.
	366th Bty. R.F.A.	LA BASSEE	ETON RD.	6.30 p.m.	ROBECQ CALONNE LESTREM PONT RIQUEL OXFORD RD ETON RD ON HEM AND CROIX	To relieve 34th Bty. To arrive after 8.30 p.m.
13th	104th Bty. R.F.A. & 8th Bty. R.F.A.	RIEZ du VINAGE	CROIX BARBEE	6.00 p.m.	CORNET MALO CTS LA CREUSE FOSSE MARLBOROUGH RD. OXFORD RD.	To arrive after 8.30
~~13th~~	~~...~~	~~...~~	~~...~~	~~8.30~~	~~CALONNE LEST...~~	~~8.30~~
13th	1 Sect 57th How Battery	ROBECQ	RUGBY ROAD	6.30 p.m.	CALONNE, LESTREM, PONT RIQUEL, PONT du HEM.	seen of
13th	16th Bty R.F.A.	BUSNES		6.30	CALONNE, ROBECQ LESTREM, PONT RIQUEL, OXFORD RD ETON RD.	To relieve 34th Bty.
	2 Sections 71st Bty R.F.A.	RIEZ du VINAGE	CROIX BARBEE		CORNET MALO, FOSSE, MARLBORO Rd OXFORD Rd	To relieve 2 Sections 64th Bty
	104th Bty R.F.A.	LA BRASSERIE	RUGBY ROAD		ROBECQ ST, VENISSE ON CORNET MALO FOSSE MARLBORO RD ON OXFORD RD.	To arrive after 8.30 p.m. To relieve 2 Sections of 81st Battery

MARCH TABLE (contnd)

DATE	UNIT	FROM	TO	TIME	ROUTE	REMARKS
14th	8th. Bty. R.F.A.	LA BRASSERIE	CROIX BARBEE	6.30 p.m.	ROBECQ MT. BERNICHON CORNET MALO FOSSE MALBOROUGH RD. OXFORD RD.	To arrive after 8.30 p.m.
14th	4th. Bde. R.F.A. Amm. Column.	RIEZ du VINAGE	R15c 3.10	8 a.m.	CORNET MALO	In sufficient time to take up the supply of 18 pr. Amm from 10 a.m on 15th. and S.A.A. according to orders received from Infantry Brigadiers
14th.	5th. Bde. R.F.A. Amm. Column.	BUSNES	R12c 5.4	8 a.m.	ROBECQ CALONNE LESTREM PONT RIQUEL	
14th.	13th. Bde. R.F.A. Amm. Column.	LA BRASSERIE.	R53b 8.6	8 a.m.	ROBECQ MT BERNICHON CORNET MALO.	
14th.	43rd. Bde. R.F.A. Amm. Column.	ROBECQ	LES LOBES	8 a.m.	MT. BERNICHON CORNET MALO	
15th.	30th (How) Bty.(less 1 Section)	ROBECQ	ST. VAAST M31d 8.8	6.30 p.m.	MT. BERNICHON CORNET MALO CIX HAMBURG FOSSE MALBOROUGH RD. OXFORD RD. CROIX BARBEE	To relieve 54th. Bty. of 1st. Division. (1 section on left 13/14
15th	37th (How) Battery 2 Sections	ROBECQ	RUGBY ROAD M22 a 2.3	6.30. AM	CALONNE, LESTREM, PONT RIQUEL, PONT An HEM	To relieve 2 sections of 93rd Battery.

Amendments to MEERUT Divisional Artillery Operation Order No. 15 dated 10-4-15

Para 3 (a) Northern Group, for 40th. (How) Btty., substitute 57th (How) Btty.
Para 3 (B) Centre Group, for 57th (How) Btty., substitute 40th (How) Btty.
Last line, for 2308 5.1 read M318 5.7

Last line, add- "FAHORE Divisional Ammunition Column is at CAIPHAR"

Amendments to "TRENCH TABLE" issued in connection with above Operation Order.

Relieved 1 section 64th. Btty. by 1 section 7th. Btty., for 15th read 19th. O.P.
15th. 1 Section 7th. Btty., under "Remarks" read as follows
       1 Section of 64th. Btty.
19th. 1 Section 64th. Btty., under "Remarks" read as follows
       1 Section of 21st. Btty.

DATE	TROOPS	FROM	TO	ROUNDS	HOURS	REMARKS
15th.	1 Section 8th. Btty.	LA BRAS-LAIS	FACIX BARBUE pos.	6:30 p.m.	RICHEBOURG, MONQUISSE, QUINCY HALL, ROUGE CROIX, NEUF CHAPELLE	

| 13th.) 14th.) | Cancel registrate of the 57th. Btty. and substitute- | | | | | |

| 15th. | 1 Section 57th.Btty. | ESTREE | RICHE BOURG & QUENTIN | 6:30 p.m. D.V. | CARNOUR, QUINCHY, NEUF PLOT, RED KM, RUE DU BOIS | Registrate CALONNE. If possible, to relieve one Section of 57th. Btty. |

| 14th. 57th. Btty., under "Remarks" for "57 Section & 2 Sect." at 64th. Btty. | | | | | | |
| ADD- 64th. Btty. | | | | | | add Section 2 Sections of 64th. Btty. |

| 15th. 57th. (How) Btty. 2 sections | ESTREE | RUGBY RD. 6:30 D.V. | | CARNOUR, QUINCHY, NEUF PLOT, RED KM, RUE DU BOIS | To relieve 2 sections 57th (How) Battery | |

Corrections entered

APPENDIX 135

S E C R E T

TACTICAL PROGRESS REPORT.

15th April 1915.

1(a) ACTION BY OUR OWN ARTILLERY

Further registration carried out by all batteries detailed as "LIASON" batteries.
40th Howitzer Battery fired a few rounds of shrapnel at enemy front trenches near Pt 130, also at working party in rear of fire trench near this point.

1(b) ACTION BY ENEMY'S ARTILLERY

4.p.m. Flashes of hostile battery firing on RUE BACQUEROT from ridge near HAUTE POMMERAU gave true bearing of flash 117° from M 29 c 9'9.

44th Battery was shelled at 12.45.p.m. by 4'2" Howitzer fuze set at 46. Probably map shooting and did not stop 44th continuing its own shoot. Only one shell fell very near the battery.

2. INFORMATION.

Considerable work reported in hostile trenches opposite "E" Section, apparently revetting.
Enemey's snipers very active opposite G Section.
Enemy reported strengthening parapet at Pt 263.
German aeroplane proceeding Northwards at 2.25.p.m. was engaged by our "Archibald"(26 rounds) and made off in N.N.E. direction. Was flying very high.

Major R.A.

Brigade Major, Royal Artillery,
MEERUT DIVISION.

16th April 1915

1st Army reports:- German L V G aeroplane observed to-day marked with White Cross on large black disc on under surface of plane.

APPENDIX 136

TACTICAL ARTILLERY REPORT
15th April 1915.

ACTION BY OUR OWN ARTILLERY
"A" Battery continued on German trenches.
4.5 Howitzer Battery shelled working parties in vicinity of point 83, where considerable activity was observed, also trenches and wire at point 130 and barricade 135.
4.5 Howitzer Battery shelled SNIPER'S HOUSE(209) at request of Brigadier of 7th Division, who are much troubled by sniping from this point. Four hits obtained. This house practically destroyed before we did not admit of very telling results.

ACTION OF HOSTILE ARTILLERY
Hostile Artillery much more active during the day.
4 A.M. German 4"5 Howitzer shelled their own trenches at point 128.
9 a.m. 4"5 Howitzer fired 12 rounds on our support trenches K 35 b 4-7.
a.m. Same battery fired a few rounds at support trenches in M 29 d a 5.
.30 to Same battery fired on trenches in M 29 b 0 2.
10.a.m.
11.a.m. Same battery on road near running from KEN(M 32 d 4 9)
.40 to Same battery on hedges in M 29 c doing good practice.
12.a.m.
.30.p.m. Same battery on line M 29 a 5 5 to M 29 a 7 10.
       This battery was now located and apparently registering.
.30.p.m. Fieldgun fired 10 H.E. on support trenches western edge of M 29 d.
.p.m. "PIPSQUEAK" fired 4 rounds into M 28 b 0 5 and just previous to this a few rounds in vicinity of 2nd Battery position.
       No blind shell observed during any of the foregoing hostile shelling from 9 a.m. to 5 p.m.
The Battery O.P. twice shelled during day- at 1.5 p.m. and 4.p.m., no direct hits being obtained.
Vicinity of FORT ARTHUR shelled by Howitzer and PIPSQUEAK at 5.p.m. from direction South of BOIS du BIEZ.
Fire trenches just in rear of point 82 shelled between 10 a.m. and 11 a.m. Infantry think fire came from FERME du PIEZ(91).
.15 p.m. to) 10 to 12 H.E. 3"-3"5 H.E. shell fell 200 to 300 yards short
.30 p.m.   ) of 70th Battery position. Hostile battery believed
) to be located in M 28 d.

INFORMATION.
Snipers were very busy during night 15th/16th opposite F sub-section and during today opposite E sub & F & ORCHARD.
Hostile O.P. located in house at point 131.
Considerable activity in neighbourhood of point 83.
Enemy observed re-building parapet 202 from 3 to 5 p.m.
Revetting was being carried out in the vicinity of 202 during the day.
Sniping takes place from houses at points 204 and 209.
At point 204 German trench was behind a hedge in front of the houses.
OBSTACLES:-Opposite point 128 there are large chevaux de frise and wire 4 feet high. Point 197-three strand fence 4 feet high.
Point 206-Trip wire 3 strands. Point 207- chevaux de frise in front, then a ditch and earth parapet in rear. A ditch and trip wire. From 203 to 209 there is trip wire.
MACHINE GUNS:- Machine guns in the communicating trench between 175 and 205. Just past 207, at first house on the right of F sub-section. Machine gun at M 29 d 0 8. German trench?
We have a post in the Communication trench between D and E (former machine gun).
REDOUBTS:- There is a possible redoubt at point 203 and one at 209.
One hostile aeroplane flew over CALONNE returning towards LILLE at 11.30.a.m.

Major R.A.

SECRET

TACTICAL PROGRESS REPORT
17th April 1915

APPENDIX 137

1(a) ACTION BY OUR OWN ARTILLERY

Further registration on more distant points carried out during the day.
At 1.30.p.m. 28th Battery shelled hostile gun position at N 31 b 5'0 and at once stopped german field battery that had opened fire.
20th Battery shelled N 31 d 5'8 and SNIPER'S House in M 30 c 8'8-
57th How: Battery fired on small White House at pt 259 by request of Infantry of G sub-section. Its colour is now yellow.
Same battery fired on Min du PIETRE obtaining 1 direct hit on the chimney with percussion and putting 2 lyddite practically in. This chimney is doubtless used both as O.P. and for sniping.
30th How: Battery at urgent request of 2nd Gurkhas endeavoured to demolish machine gun S.W. of barricade on LA BASSEE Road.
2nd Siege Battery registered FERME du BIEZ, 2nd round a direct hit, causing a big conflagration. A continuous crackle ensued indicating destruction of store of S.A.A. there. This lasted 12 minutes. Same battery registered point 60.
At 3.15.p.m. 8th Battery fired at enemy moving in communicating trench at S 11 a 5'2.
40th How: Battery fired at enemy working party constructing dug out at pt 63 at 12.5.p.m., 2.p.m. and 3.30.p.m.
7th Battery shelled trenches opposite "C" sub-section in retaliation of shelling our trenches there at 2.p.m.

1(b) ACTION BY HOSTILE ARTILLERY

3.4.a.m. "Bomb Guns" active opposite section "E". Infantry report two of these in trench S.W. of pts 203 and 204.
6.45.a.m. 4'2" How: fired 8 rounds at Brewery at NEUVE CHAPELLE.
6.50 to 7.a.m. PIPSQUEAK active on MIN farm.
7.5 to 7.15.a.m. 4'2" How: shelled support trenches in M 28 b 5'5 and M 29 c 8'7- Battery believed to be in direction of N 32 d.
7.25 to 8.5.a.m. PIPSQUEAK shelled along RUE de BACQUEROT.
7.30 to 8.50.a.m. What is reported as a 4" gun shelled billet at M 21 d 10'3- 50 to 60 H.E. shell, of which 14 were direct hits. Shell groove in front of Farm gave magnetic bearing of 125°.
10.55.a.m. 4'2" How: from direction of S 6 b 5'5 shelled our support trenches about M 35 a 7'7 and round M 35 a 7'0 to M 35 c 7'7 at 11.30.a.m
12 to 12.20.p.m. Field guns from about N 32 d shelled road about M 15 c 8'7 probably seeing wagons moving along road at that time.
4.50.p.m. CRESCENT trench shelled by Howitzer Battery apparently from S 17 a.
5.40.p.m. PIPSQUEAK located (approx) at S 16 d 9'2 by flashes, was active.

2. INFORMATION

Snipers appear to have been quiet on front of BAREILLY Brigade during night 16th/17th.
Moral effect of shelling of pt 263 (SNIPER'S House) by 57th Howitzer Battery yesterday appears to have been good.
Sniping very heavy opposite ORCHARD during the day.
OBSTACLES:- There is Chevaux de Frise from N.E. to S.E. of our advanced post 196 and entanglements continue S.W. on high angle-iron posts and low wooden stakes; the wire crossed.
MACHINE GUNS:- There is a machine gun emplacement in trench at pt 197, which shoots N.W. This gun is concealed by 3 dark coloured sandbags during the day.
A machine gun is S.W. of barricade on la BASSEE road in an emplacement jutting out from the front trench.
There are gaps in hedge S.W. of road passing through pts 203 204, presumably made for bomb guns to fire through- these are occasionally blocked up.
Heavy traffic heard on road in front of BOIS du BIEZ about 10.p.m., and two of our field batteries shelled this road.

No hostile aircraft seen to-day.

Major R.A.

Brigade Major, Royal Artillery,
MEERUT DIVISION.

SECRET.

APPENDIX 138

TACTICAL PROGRESS REPORT
18th April 1915.

1(a) ACTION BY OUR OWN ARTILLERY
2.30.p.m. 20th Battery fired on enemy's trenches in G sub-section and on working parties.
57th How: Battery registered on houses behind enemy front line trenches
3.10.p.m. 8th Battery fired on working party in trench S 11 a 3'2- enemy fled.
4.25.p.m. 4th Brigade batteries fired few rounds on enemy trenches to keep down hostile rifle fire on our aeroplanes. Same Brigade fired on following working parties:-
    2.p.m. & 3.30.p.m. Communicating trench near point 139.
    3.30.p.m.,4.15.p.m.,5.30.p.m. at point 63.
    4.45.p.m. 150 yards N.E. of point 51, behind fire trench.
    6.10.p.m. 14th Battery fired on party of men going down communicating trench point 57.

1(b) ACTION BY HOSTILE ARTILLERY.
Enemy artillery much quieter to-day.
7.15.a.m. Field battery fired 3 rounds 200 yards short of 28th Battery- all 3 were "blind".
10.20 a.m. to 11.40.a.m. German field gun(yesterday reported at N 31 b 5'10 but now ▇▇▇ believed to be more N.E. of that) opened fire on cross roads M 22 b 9'5(RUE BACQUEROT) then searched up to 28th Battery position and across roads at ▇▇▇ M 15 a 9'5.
11.a.m. German 4" gun joined in and fired on the latter vicinity. These are thought to be the same batteries that shelled 57th Battery billet yesterday, from direction N 31 b 5'0, as direction and fuzes corresponden.
6.30.p.m. 6 rounds from light howitzer fired at cross roads M 35 a 7'3.

2. INFORMATION.
Intermittent rifle and machine gun fire night 17th/18th to cover working parties- and from 2.a.m. to 4.a.m. to-day.

MACHINE GUNS.
Hostile machine guns have been located at points 141 and 206, the former is removed during the day.

OBSTACLES.
Wire entanglement near M 30 c 6'5 is being strengthened.
A lot of the wire opposite "G" Sub-section is old and rusty!
Every few yards along fire trench opposite NEUVE CHAPELLE are loopholes, which could be used for machine guns- none however were located.

SNIPING.
Heavy sniping still goes on about O.P. in front of "Good Luck House", many German periscopes were seen there.
Following hostile aircraft were seen:-
    7.50.a.m. Aeroplane sighted at bearing 115° flying high and out of range, turned in N.N.E. direction.
    9.14.a.m. MORANE(German) flying high, bearing 250°, engaged and turned N.N.E. by our Archibald.
    9.50.a.m. AVIATIC flying high, bearing 200° was engaged and turned in Easterly direction.
    4.23.p.m. German aeroplane reported flying up and down our lines(?)
2nd Battery R.F.A. assisted Archibald to-day with telephonic observations from the trenches, with excellent results.

R.F. Lynch-Staunton.
Major R.A.

Brigade Major, Royal Artillery,
MEERUT DIVISION.

APPENDIX 139

Report on entanglements etc on the front from near point 63 to point V6 by 30th Howitzer Battery R.F.A. 19th April 1915.

The wire on the enemy's front line in front of our zone is for the most part very thick. In many places old and rusty wire has been strongly reinforced with new wire. At two places however the wire is very scanty and thin, namely (1) for about 60 yards just S.W. of point 59; (2) for about 50 yards midway between points 59 and 60. Here the wire is very old and rusty. On the rest of the front the wire consists in some places of Chevaux de Frise and in others of coils of wire on stakes of wood and iron, while in many places there is a combination of entanglements and Chevaux de Frise.

Near point 60 and from about midway between points 59 and V6 to point V6 the parapet is very strongly built up with sandbags. Steel loophole plates are very frequent indeed. Most of them might conceal machine guns. At point 60 just W. of the LA BASSEE Road there is a strongly built advanced work, obviously a machine gun emplacement. About two thirds of the way between points 59 and V6 a telephone wire supported on sticks can be seen coming forward to the front line. At this point periscopes are always much in evidence. This seems a very likely place for an Artillery Forward Officer.

The only obstacle between our front line and the German wire is the remains of a hedge running just in front of our front line. The Infantry should be able to supply accurate information as to the character of this obstacle.

No. 569-R.A.(L). Headquarters Divisional Artillery,
MEERUT DIVISION.

20th April 1915.

To,
 The GENERAL STAFF, MEERUT DIVISION.
 The G.O.C., R.A., LAHORE DIVISION,

Forwarded for information.

Major R.A.
for Commanding Royal Artillery,
MEERUT DIVISION.

SECRET

APPENDIX 140

TACTICAL PROGRESS REPORT
19th April 1915.
▼▼▼▼▼▼▼▼▼▼▼▼▼▼▼▼▼▼▼▼▼▼▼▼▼▼▼▼▼▼▼▼▼▼▼▼

1(a) ACTION BY OUR OWN ARTILLERY

Further registration proceeded with.
12.30.a.m. 8th Battery fired on enemy's trenches to retaliate for those of the 2nd 8th Gurkhas being shelled.
11.30.a.m. 5th Howitzer Battery fired on point 203, where working parties were reported making emplacements for bomb guns.
11.45.a.m. 30th How: Battery fired to stop "Bombing" in ORCHARD Trench. Same battery fired on machine gun by barricade on LA BASSEE Road, N. of point 60, which had caused a lot of trouble to our Infantry. Also supposed O.P's at points 53 and V 10., hostile shelling of CRESCENT trench ceased when latter was shelled.
4th Brigade batteries registered supposed O.P's at points 50,51 and 125 also at S 5 d 10'9, snipers house at 125, and put 3 good rounds into strong working party in fire trench S 11 b.

1(b) ACTION BY HOSTILE ARTILLERY

8.20.a.m. O.P. in NEUVE CHAPELLE was shelled by 4'2" Howitzers from direction S 6 b 5'5.
8.44.a.m. PIPSQUEAK active from S 17 a on our trenches.
11.a.m. CRESCENT trench shelled by PIPSQUEAK.
11.15.a.m. 1 shrapnel shell fired near ROUGE CROIX.
11.25.a.m. 1 heavy H.E. shell fell near NEUVE CHAPELLE and some rounds near houses at M 23 b 4'3.
11.30.a.m. CROIX BARBEE shelled by light howitzers.
11.50.a.m. F Sub-section trenches shelled by 4'2" Howitzer.
11.55.a.m. Same battery fired 5 rounds near M 21 d 8'2 it is believed to be in N 31 b 5'8.
12.15.p.m. PIPSQUEAK from direction of AUBERS fired 4 rounds at 57th Battery billet.
3.5.p.m. PIPSQUEAK fired 6 rounds on the MIN M 22 d 2'4, obtaining 1 direct hit.
3.15.p.m. Our reserve trenches in M 34 b 4'7 shelled by German How: Battery from direction N 31 b.
3.35.p.m. Enemy fired 5 H.E. shell at cross roads M 15 c 7'7.
7.p.m. Enemy fired 4 large bombs into salient trench from point 204, 2nd Battery stopped the bombing with 2 rounds.

2. INFORMATION

Enemy's artillery active again during the day.
Our new trench from M 29 b 8'7 to M 24 c 3'2 completed last night.
Enemy have a Sap running a short way out from point 257.
Large German working party seen in support trenches in S 11 d about 3.p.m.
IDENTIFICATION:- One HUN seen with a light blue cap in trench at pt 61.
SNIPING:- In Southern Section much diminished.
Snipers were seen firing at 5.15.p.m. from L shaped house S.W. of point 125, which is also probably an O.P. This ceased when a battery opened fire on this house.
BOMBING:- At 11.50.a.m. 12 to 15 Germans noticed in Redoubt in S 10 d 5'8. These commenced bombing our trenches in reply to our bombing. They were sent to ground by 3 rounds from 2nd Siege and a field battery Smoke from the Bomb thrower when fired was distinctly visible.
ORCHARD trench bombed 3 times during the day-11.45.a.m.,4.45.p.m. and 5.25.p.m.
OBSTACLES:- Earthwork at S 11 c 1'7 protected by low wire entanglement made of very rusty wire. Zig Zag communicating trench leads from it to front line trench.
Low sticks for wire entanglement have been erected behind trench from point 129 to 139.
There is "trip" wire behind fire trench point 127 to point 129.
MACHINE GUNS:- One located near point 141.
Battery located near S 6 b 5'5. "Boom" gun emplacement built at pt 203.
HOSTILE AEROPLANES:- 10.47.a.m. one sighted flying high and out of range magnetic bearing 140°, turned E. 10.57.am. one sighted flying high magnetic bearing 350°, out of range, turned N.N.E.

Major R.A.
Brigade Major, Royal Artillery,
MEERUT DIVISION.

Copy No. 5
APPENDIX 140a

OPERATION ORDER NO. 27,

By

Lieutenant-General Sir C. A. ANDERSON, K.C.B.,

Commanding MEERUT Division.

20th April 1915.

Reference — BOIS DU BIEZ Map 1/10000
and Map of FRANCE 1/40000.

Intention. 1. Under instructions from 1st Army, the 4th Corps will take over the front of the Indian Corps as far south as the road 121-140-142 exclusive.

Reliefs. 2. The MEERUT Division will be relieved from the front line on the nights 24th/25th and 25th/26th April as follows :—

BAREILLY Brigade by 22nd Brigade, 7th Division.
DEHRA DUN Brigade by FEROZEPORE Brigade, LAHORE Division.
GARHWAL Brigade, by SIRHIND Brigade, LAHORE Division.

Details connected with reliefs will be arranged direct between Brigade Commanders concerned.
All movements will be made as in attached March Table.
Brigade Commanders will hand over command of their Sections as the relief of their troops is completed, reporting at once to Divisional Headquarters.

Machine Guns. 3. Machine Guns of No. 5 Motor Machine Gun Battery, 4th Indian Cavalry and 107th Pioneers, will be withdrawn from the line on the night 25th/26th April.

4th Indian Cavalry. 4. 4th Indian Cavalry will exchange billets with 15th Indian Lancers on the afternoon of 23rd April.

Artillery. 5. The Artillery of the MEERUT Division will remain in the line and come under the orders of G.O.C. LAHORE Division. The LAHORE Divisional Ammunition Column will supply ammunition.

S. & Ms. and 107th Pioneers. 6. Nos. 3 and 4 Companies, 1st S. & Ms., and the 107th Pioneers, will remain in their present billets.

Medical. 7. Field Ambulances will be relieved on the 26th April under arrangements to be made direct by A.Ds. M.S., LAHORE and MEERUT Divisions.

Refilling. 8. The GARHWAL Brigade will exchange Refilling Point with the SIRHIND Brigade on 24th April.
The DEHRA DUN Brigade will exchange Refilling Point with the FEROZEPORE Brigade on the 26th April.
The Refilling Points of the BAREILLY Brigade and Divisional Troops will not change.
Refilling on 23rd April will be as at present.
Details of refilling on 24th, 25th and 26th April, will be issued separately.

Train. 9. No. 3 Company of Divisional Train will exchange billets with the SIRHIND Brigade Train Company on the 23rd April, marching with its Brigade.
No. 2 Company of Divisional Train will exchange billets with FEROZEPORE Brigade Train Company after refilling on 25th April.
The Headquarter Company of the Train and No. 4 Company will stand fast in present billets.

2.

Billetting Areas. 10. The attached tracing placed over Map Sheets 36 and 36A,1/40000, shows the new Indian Corps' and LAHORE and MEERUT Divisional areas.

Command. 11. G.O.C., MEERUT Division will hand over command of the front line at 8.0 a.m., on 26th April 1915.

                                               C. Norie, Colonel,
General Staff, MEERUT Division.

Issued at 6.0 p.m. by Signal Company.

```
Copy No.  1  to Indian Corps.
          2     Lahore Division
          3     First Division
          4     Seventh Division
          5     C. R. A., MEERUT Division
          6     Dehra Dun Bde
          7     Garhwal Bde
          8     Bareilly Bde
          9     4th Ind. Cavalry
         10     107th Indian Pioneers
         11     C.R.E. Meerut Divn
         12     Signal Coy, Meerut Div.
         13     Meerut Div. Train
         14     No. 5 Motor M.Gun Battery
         15     A.A. & Q.M.G.   Meerut
         16     D.A.A.G.          do.
         17     D.A.A. & Q.M.G.   do.
         18     A.D.M.S. Meerut
         19 )
         20 )  War Diary and files.
         21 )
         22 )
```

March Table (contd)

1	2	3	4	5	6
April 25th & night 25/26th	2 Bns BAREILLY Bde	REZ BAILLEUL	Area No. 7	MALVERN ROAD, CAMBRIDGE Road, FOSSE, La CIX MARMUSE, LE CORNET MALO.	To pass FOSSE Bridge at 12.30 p.m.
April 25th & night 25/26th	DEHRA DUN Bde (less 2 battns)	Trenches Centre Section	Area No. 2	PONT LOGY, ROUGE CROIX, CROIX BARBEE, LACOUTURE, VIEILLE CHAPELLE, ZELOBES.	LOCON -- LESTREM Road to be cleared by 3.0 a.m.
April 25th & night 25/26th	BAREILLY Bde (less 2 battns)	Trenches Northern Section	Area No. 7	RUE DU BACQUEROT, PONT DU HEM, BOUT DEVILLE, FOSSE, Bridge, ZELOBES.	do. do.

Note:- In the above table, the billeting area now occupied by Sirhind Bde around CALONNE is referred to as No.1
  Ferozepore Bde   PARADIS   No.2
  Jullundur Bde   CIX MARMUSE   No.3
  Garhwal Bde   VIEILLE CHAPELLE No.4
  Dehra Dun Bde   Centre Sect.trenches No.5
  Bareilly Bde   Northern do. do. No.6
  New area in vicinity of)
  LESLOBES and LE CORNET)   No.7
  MALO

SECRET.
APPENDIX 141

TACTICAL PROGRESS REPORT
20th April 1915

1(a) ACTION BY OUR OWN ARTILLERY

4.10.a.m. to 5.30.a.m. 9th Brigade batteries registered hostile trenches on their immediate front. Same Brigade also registered the following points during the day.
186, MOULIN du PIETRE, 362, 290, 204 this latter being reported as exact position of "bomb guns" the point is 85 yds W. of and 15 yds S. of centre of 204.
4th Brigade batteries registered points 69, fire trench E. of 33 FERME du BIEZ, house at point 121 in which enemy were seen.
12.20.p.m. Large working parties between 130 and 131 was shelled.
4.15.p.m. Enemy's infantry who were firing on our aeroplane were shelled by us.
4.p.m. 8th Battery shelled working party at S 11 a 3˙2.
5.p.m. 8th Battery fired at Distillery and obtained 2 direct hits.

1(b) ACTION BY HOSTILE ARTILLERY

9.15.a.m. to 9.45.a.m. German howitzer shelled houses at M 23 d.
9.45.a.m. German field gun shelled support trenches in "C" Sub-section and communicating trench in M 29 c - probably from direction N 31 b 4˙
10.a.m. 5'9" How: shelled CHAPIGNY.
11.15.a.m. Field gun shelled communication trench in "B" Sub-section, and 12.20.p.m. same battery fired 9 rounds on vicinity M 29 a 1 2.
12.35.p.m. How: fired 6 rounds across road at M 15 a 9˙2.
12.55.p.m. PIPSQUEAK shelled RUE de BACAURET in M 22 b from the direction of LES MOTTES Fme.
1.30.p.m. Heavy 5'9" (75") shells fell near position of 87th Battery.
1.45.p.m. 25 5'9" How: shell put into St VAAST, RICHEBOURG and 2nd Siege Battery's Headquarters.
1.55.p.m. German 4'2" How: fired 5 H.E. shell near the MIN M 23 d.
2.15.p.m. Same battery dropped 1percuss at road junction M 15 c 7˙7 and 1 H.E. S. of the MIN.
2.10.p.m. Same battery shelled road junction M 15 c 7˙7 and cross roads at PONT du HEM.
4.p.m. Brewery in NEUVE CHAPELLE shelled, Major and 1 subaltern 88th Battery slightly wounded. This building was shelled at intervals all through the day.
4.15.p.m. PIPSQUEAK shelled CRESCENT trench.
5.45.p.m. 5'9" How: fired 3 rds in vicinity of 87th Battery.
6.p.m. Howitzer Battery shelled houses in M 15 b 9˙4.

2. INFORMATION

Enemy's artillery far more active again to-day, especially about observing stations.
"MOTHER" destroyed the chimney of the MOULIN du PIETRE at 2.30.p.m. at the 5th round.
IDENTIFICATION:- HUNS seen in trench at S 11 a 9˙9 wearing new dark blue uniforms, some with light blue collars.
FLASHES:- Believed to have been located at T 2 d 2˙2 ARMY and M 27 d 6˙2.
BOMBING:- Took place at 10.a.m. to right of ORCHARD trench. Our bomb guns competed with this. The Bomb fired at our Salient trench on night 19th/20th is described as a heavy, cylindrical bomb, about 5 inches in diameter and 12 ins long, bursting by a time fuze.
SNIPING: Less to-day at CRESCENT trench, but very bad at NEUVE CHAPELLE especially from large "T" shaped house S.E. of point 125. 7th Divisional Artillery report 2 houses each side point 280, and haystack between 282 and 280 much used by snipers to enfilade the 7th Division trenches.
OBSTACLES:- Point 263, is very strongly sand-bagged. Many iron plated loop-holes visible. On N.W. face of it is "Apron" wire and high and low wire. There are some Farm chairs supporting some of the high wire, also plough shares amongst the wire.
Then to point 257, which has opposite it chevaux de frise, low wire and

and trip wire. At this point the sand-bag parapet is in bad repair, as are also the wire obstacles.

Opposite DEHRA DUN Brigade:- Wire appears to be of a fairly uniform type, viz. from 3 to 5 rows of posts, with in parts the row next the trench of 4 foot iron posts, say 12 to 15 yards broad. There appears to be no effort to conceal the wire. A portion midway between points 51 and 63 is invisible from S 4 d 1.8. Some of the wire near point 56 is said to be like the French wire. From points 183 to 56 wire is of uniform type with 5 rows of posts i.e., about 30 yards deep.

HOSTILE AEROPLANES

3.p.m. AVIATIK bearing 125°, high, turned E, to bearing 90°, came over three times, was engaged and 83 rounds fired at it, last seen 4.p.m. travelling S.E.

4.50.p.m. AVIATIK, bearing 105°, high, engaged with 16 rounds, turned in S.E. direction.

5.15.p.m. AVIATIK, high, bearing 125°, out of range, turned N.E.

5.55.p.m. AVIATIK, high, bearing 195°, engaged 21 rounds turned N.E.

5.55.p.m. AVIATIK, high, bearing 88°, turned N.E. out of range.

6.3.p.m. FOKKER, high, bearing 0°, one round fired, out of range, turned N.N.E.

German Sausage Balloons seen at 1.45.p.m., true bearing 144° 30', 2 others at 4.15.p.m. true bearing 188° and 198° from M 31 b 9.7.

Major R.A.

Brigade Major, Royal Artillery,
MEERUT DIVISION.

SECRET.

TACTICAL PROGRESS REPORT
21st April 1915

1(a) ACTION BY OUR OWN ARTILLERY

Enemy's bomb guns which were active several times during the night 20th/21st at points 204,265 and opposite "C" Section were silenced each time they opened fire by field batteries.
Hostile wire and front line trenches engaged by batteries all along the front soon after dawn.
The following objectives were engaged during the day by field batteries unless otherwise stated:-
  Snipers on haystack at point 260.
  Trenches near point 204 to stop bombing by field battery and Heavy.
  Point 260 and MEW du PELTRE. Point 262 by Howtizers.
  Trenches opposite "C" section to stop rifle fire at our aeroplane.
  Trench from V2 to N.14.c.1.0 was registered. Houses near C.
  Enemy's Infantry who were watching NEUVE CHAPELLE being shelled.
  House at 184, four hits obtained.
  Working parties between 65 and 66.
  184 and 125 by field battery in conjunction with Heavies.
  Party of Germans in communicating trench behind 260.
  Germans in fire trench near 51.   House   R 16
  20 Germans in 5.11 b. effect good.

(b) ACTION BY HOSTILE ARTILLERY

Heavy How. shelled LA BASSEE Road E. of FORT du NIR about 10 a.m. from direction of AUBERS.
10.5 cm. How. shelled reserve trenches N 36 a from direction of HAUTE POMMERAU about 10.15 a.m.
15 cm. How. tried to hit house at N 27 b 4 2 from 10.40 to 10.50 a.m.
77 mm. battery shelled main road E. of ROUGE CROIX
10.5 cm. How. set a house at ROUGE CROIX on fire at 2.15 p.m.
77 mm. battery shelled BOIS du BOIS about 11.30 a.m.South from direction
15 cm. How. shelled BOIS du BOIS about 12 noon   BOIS du BOIS.
15 cm. How. shelled N 32 d 7.7 at 3.45 p.m.
10.5 cm. How. shelled near FONT du HEM 4.15 p.m.
15 cm. How.) Shelled NEUVE CHAPELLE and FAUQUIRS from 2.30 also the
10.5 cm. How.)
77 mm Guns)9.50.a.m. and intermittently throughout the day.
15 cm. How. fired 3 or 4 rounds into N 26 a.

2.   INFORMATION

Fresh wire entanglements being put up in front of 140 supported on upright iron stakes 5 feet high.
A machine gun has been located 20 yards E. of 140 at foot of big tree
A new work at 250 has been commenced. Sandbags and wooden pieces are being used. It is not certain what the work is meant to be.
Sniping on the CRESCENT trench throughout the day was very heavy.
Germans bombed near the ORCHARD trench about noon.
Entanglements in front of salient near point 65, front line trench is of iron wire, very closely interwoven and apparently rusty. It is 15 to 20 feet in depth and appears a very formidable obstacle.
No hostile aeroplanes were seen to-day
A certain amount of movement was heard near 204 during the night.

Major R.A.
Brigade Major, Royal Artillery,
FIRST DIVISION.

SECRET.

TACTICAL PROGRESS REPORT
22nd April 1915.

APPENDIX 142

1(a) ACTION BY OUR OWN ARTILLERY

3.30.a.m. All batteries of Northern Section opened fire on hostile trenches, according to previous agreement with G.O.C. BAREILLY Brigade, which opened heavy musketry fire from 3.15 to 3.30.a.m.
5.a.m. 30th How: Battery registered the Distillery.
8.a.m. 30th How: Battery retaliated to hostile shelling of our trenches, by doing likewise. Hostile fire ceased.
11.a.m. Trenches from point 128 to point 131 were shelled by 4th Bde.
11.15.a.m. 20th Battery fired 6 rounds at Cross Roads in N 25 b 3'3 where several Germans were seen.
11.15.a.m. 8th Battery fired a few rounds at the Chateau in S 17 a 7'7.
11.30.a.m. and) 19th and 28th Batteries carried out registration in
12.45.p.m.   ) their new zones.
11.40.a.m. House at 65 reported as O.P. was shelled.
3.p.m. 57th How: Battery shelled houses from point 202 to point 146 at request of Infantry of "E" Sub-section.
3.15.p.m. 20th Battery shelled sniper's house at haystack near point 260.
4.35.p.m. 57th How: Battery fired on houses in vicinity of point 204 by special request of Infantry. House indicated was burnt to the ground and two more close by set alight.
The 108th Heavy Battery shelled house at point 69, observation by 66th Battery's Observing Officer.
2nd and 5th Siege Batteries commenced registration.

1(b) ACTION BY HOSTILE ARTILLERY

Hostile batteries were very quiet on the whole to-day.
7.45.a.m. PORT ARTHUR shelled by 10'5 cm. Howitzers and PIPSQUEAK.
During the morning hostile artillery were shelling their own trench just S. of point 56, apparently with a view of registration. They also registered ORCHARD Redoubt which they have not done before.
1.p.m. 6 "Black Marias" (21 cm. Hows) fell in PORT ARTHUR.
5.10.p.m. Our trenches in front of points 130 and 133 were shelled.
5.30 to 6.p.m. 10'5 cm. fired about 8 rounds close to the 44th Battery position.
6.15.p.m. Hostile flashes seen at N 26 o 6'5.
6.40.p.m. 3 "Black Marias" (21 cm.) fell near road at M 16 a 7'8.
7.p.m. Same battery shelled vicinity of M 16 c 1'1 from direction of HERLIES?
Brewery and neighbourhood in NEUVE CHAPELLE shelled at intervals during day by PIPSQUEAK and also some heavy gun.

2. INFORMATION

OBSTACLES:- Wire at house 69 which had been knocked down by our heavy batteries yesterday, was replaced during night 21st/22nd.
COMMUNICATION TRENCH is being dug from "G" Sub section to "MOATED GRANGE".
SNIPING:- Much less troublesome to-day, doubtless due to much increased energy of our own men in this direction, especially in the Southern Section.
SINGING:- Much singing and shouting was reported in the German lines during the night.
HOSTILE AEROPLANES:- 11.15.a.m. AVIATIK sighted, high, bearing 150°, engaged 4 rounds, turned E. and was then out of range.
4.15.p.m. AVIATIK, high, bearing 40°, engaged 26 rounds, turned S.E.
5.55.p.m. AVIATIK, high, bearing 150°, out of range, turned East.

R.H. Lynch-Staunton,
Major R.A.

Brigade Major, Royal Artillery,
MEERUT DIVISION.

APPENDIX 144.

Copy No. 16

OPERATION ORDER No.16
by
Brigadier General R.St.C. LECKY, R.A. C.R.A. MEERUT Division.

Reference:-
Map FRANCE 1/40,000. 23rd April 1915.

INTENTION. 1. The 4th Corps will take over the front of the INDIAN Corps as far South as road 121-140-142 inclusive.

RELIEFS. 2. The MEERUT Division will be relieved from the front line on the nights 24th/25th and 25th/26th April as follows:-
BAREILLY Brigade by 22nd Brigade, 7th Division.
DEHRA DUN Brigade by FEROZEPORE Brigade, LAHORE Division.
GARHWAL Brigade by SIRHIND Brigade, LAHORE Division.
G.O.C. MEERUT Division will hand over command of front line at 6.a.m. on 26th April.

ARTILLERY. 3. The Artillery of the MEERUT Division with 43rd (Howitzer) Brigade R.F.A. and 8th Brigade R.G.A. will remain in action for the defence of the INDIAN Corps front.

ARTILLERY RELIEFS. 4. 9th Brigade R.F.A. will be relieved by two batteries, 2nd West Riding Field Artillery Brigade on nights 22nd/23rd to 25th/26th April in accordance with instructions already issued and will move into positions in M 20 and M 27.
O.C. 9th Brigade R.F.A. will hand over the command of the Artillery of the Northern Section to O.C. 2nd West Riding Field Artillery Brigade at 6.a.m. 25th April.
Headquarters 2nd West Riding F.A. Bde will be at M 4 c 1'1.
Headquarters 22nd Brigade will be at M 4 c 4'3.

ARTILLERY GROUPS. 5. The present Centre Group R.A.-O.C. Colonel L.A.C. GORDON, R.F.A. will become the new Northern Group and will be grouped with the FEROZEPORE Brigade. Headquarters . . .
The present Southern Group R.A.-O.C. Lt Colonel P.A. TYLER, R.F.A. with the addition of the 2nd Battery R.F.A. will become the new Southern Group and will be grouped with the SIRHIND Brigade. Headquarters those of the GARHWAL Bde.
The remainder of the MEERUT Divisional Artillery will be under the direct control of G.O.C., R.A., MEERUT Division.

AMMUNITION. 6. MEERUT Division Brigade Ammunition Columns will continue to supply S.A.A. to the same Infantry Brigades of the MEERUT Division as they are supplying at present.
LAHORE Divisional Ammunition Column at CALONNE will continue to supply ammunition to all troops in the front line.

COMMAND. 7. G.O.C., R.A., MEERUT Division will remain in command of the Artillery, as detailed above, on the INDIAN Corps front under the G.O.C., LAHORE Division. Position of Headquarters of MEERUT Division and of MEERUT Divisional Artillery will remain as at present.
Headquarters of LAHORE Division will be in GRAND RUE, ESTAIRES and of the LAHORE Divisional Artillery at VEILLE CHAPELLE
G.O.C., R.A., 7th Division will take over command of Artillery on front taken over by 7th Division at 6.a.m. on 25th April.

Major R.A.
Brigade Major, Royal Artillery,
MEERUT DIVISION.

Issued at 1.30.p.m. by
Motor cyclist.

Copy No. 1 to General Staff, MEERUT Division. Copy No.14 to O.C. 6th Bde
" No. 2 to General Staff, LAHORE Division. R.G.A.
" No. 3 to G.O.C., R.A., LAHORE Division. " No.15 to O.C. MEERUT Divi
" No. 4 to G.O.C., R.A., 7th Division. Ammunition Column
" No. 5 to G.O.C. BAREILLY Brigade. " No.16 to WAR DIARY.
" No. 6 to G.O.C. GARHWAL Brigade. " No.17 to File.
" No. 7 to G.O.C. DEHRA DUN Brigade.
" No. 8 to G.O.C. FEROZEPORE Brigade.
" No. 9 to G.O.C. SIRHIND Brigade.
" No.10 to O.C. 4th Brigade R.F.A.
" No.11 to O.C. 9th Brigade R.F.A.
" No.12 to O.C. 13th Brigade R.F.A.
" No.13 to O.C. 43rd How. Bde R.F.A.

SECRET.   APPENDIX 145.

TACTICAL PROGRESS REPORT
23rd April 1915.

1(a) ACTION BY OUR OWN ARTILLERY
   10.45.a.m. Two rounds were fired at enemy O.P. at point 69 to stop PIPSQUEAK firing on our trenches.
   11.a.m. 6th Battery West Riding Brigade carried out registration on points in "E" and "F" Sub-sections, including 146 and 204.
   5th Battery same Brigade registered on points in "G" and "H" Sub-sections.
   2.15.p.m. 28th Battery registered on points 48, 68 and 18.
   3.15.p.m. A few rounds were fired at movement in house at point 63.
   14th Battery registered point 123.

1(b) ACTION BY HOSTILE ARTILLERY.
   Hostile Artillery very quiet on the whole.
   9.a.m. 10'5 CM. howitzer shelled house at road junction at M 32 d 8'2 from S.E.
   10'48.a.m. 77 mm. fired a few rounds at 66th Battery's O.P. and trenches in front of it.
   11.a.m. 10'5 cm. howitzer shelled the MIN from the direction of AUBERS.
   Only a few rounds fired into NEUVE CHAPELLE to-day.
   2.10.p.m. PIPSQUEAK shelled vicinity of M 27 b 8'2.
   2.45.p.m. 10'5 cm. Howitzer shelled house in RUE du BOIS about 120 yards W. of RITZ.
   6.15.p.m. 13 rounds 15 cm. Howitzer shell fell round about 44th Battery and DEHRA DUN Brigade Headquarters. Bearing of battery taken from M 31 d 6'8 131°- direction of ILLIES(Approx).

2.   INFORMATION.
   HOSTILE TRAFFIC:- The noise of heavy traffic noticed between 8.p.m. and 11.p.m. on night 22nd/23rd is thought to be that of traffic going along road MOULIN du PIETRE- M 36 a - N 31 d - N 31 c and then in a N.E. direction.
   AIRCRAFT:- No hostile aircraft were seen to-day.
   MACHINE GUN located 50 yards S.W. of point 146, and very active during the night.
   WORK:- Work was observed going on in front German trench at S 10 b 6'2 during the morning.
   A machine gun emplacement is apparently being made to cover ground in direction of PORT ARTHUR.
   OBSTACLES:- A good deal of work going on wire entanglement near point 204 last night.
   Each line of German trench has wire entanglement i.e. main lines- Confirmation and further particulars are required.

                                                            Major R.A.
                                         Brigade Major, Royal Artillery,
                                                       MEERUT DIVISION.

"A" Form.
MESSAGES AND SIGNALS.
Army Form C. 2121.

Prefix	Code	m.	Words	Charge	This message is on a/c of:	Recd. at	m.
Office of Origin and Service Instructions			Sent			Date	
			At	m.	Service.	From	
			To		(Signature of "Franking Officer.")	By	
			By				

TO: O.C. RA Northern Section

Sender's Number.	Day of Month.	In reply to Number	AAA
718 RA(L)	23		

Ref Operation Order 16 para 2 the DEHRA DUN and GARHWAL bde will not be relieved for the present AAA BAREILLY relief and your relief will take place as arranged

From: BMRA
Place:
Time: 4-35 pm

APPENDIX 146.

SECRET.

TACTICAL PROGRESS REPORT.
24th April 1915.

1(a) ACTION BY OUR OWN ARTILLERY

23.4.15-8.50.p.m. 2nd Battery retaliated on house 141 to "bombing" of our "listening post" at M 35 d 4.8 from trenches behind this house.
24.4.15-2.50.a.m. 2nd Battery replied to the "bombing" of our "SALIENT" trench from a point 50 yards S. of road from point 204.
4.a.m. 28th Battery fired 3 rounds on to enemy trenches in "H" Sub-section.
9.a.m. 44th Battery fired a few rounds into German trenches, to stop rifle fire on our aeroplane.
11.30.a.m. 8th Battery registered trench 54 to S 11 c 9.6.
12 noon. 5th Siege Battery registered points 52 and 63.
12.6.p.m. 7th Battery fired a few rounds at point 139.
12.50.p.m. 4th Battery registered points 140 to 204.
1.45.p.m. 19th Battery registered LIGNY LE PETIT and trenches in S 11 d.
3.30.p.m. 8th Battery fired a few rounds at machine gun emplacement at point 59 by request O.C. London Regiment.
3.50.p.m. 30th How: Battery stopped "Bombing" in ORCHARD trench by 2 rounds lyddite.
4.p.m. 14th Battery registered fire trench in front of point 66 and shelled working party in communication trench.
4.15.p.m. 44th Battery shelled house V.8. in conjunction with 48th Heavy Battery which secured 5 direct hits.
2nd Siege Battery registered on 2 houses North of LA TOURELLE cross roads.
4.30.p.m. 57th How: Battery shelled point 204 by request of "E" Sub-section. This point gives trouble every night with bomb guns.

1(b) ACTION BY HOSTILE ARTILLERY

Hostile guns exceptionally quiet to-day.
11.40.a.m. German 15 cm. Howitzer dropped 2 rounds near cross roads at M 15 c.
1.25 to 1.40.p.m. Enemy shelled NEUVE CHAPELLE and 7th Battery O.P.
3.45.p.m. Germans "bombed" our front trenches opposite "Good Luck House" and shelled CRESCENT Trench and RUE du BOIS with PIPSQUEAK from direction of V.8.
4 to 4.30.p.m. PORT ARTHUR and RUE du BOIS as far as S 9 d shelled by PIPSQUEAK and 10'5 cm. howitzers.

2. INFORMATION

MACHINE GUN:- firing from point 59 at 9.30.a.m.
LISTENING POST is reported at point 257.
AEROPLANE- AVIATIK seen at 8.30.a.m. flying high and out of range, it turned E. and returned to enemy lines.
WORK:- Extensive wood work is going on in the trenches in "H" Sub-section.
A new work has begun with overhead cover consisting of heavy beams and earth near point 58.
New wire entanglement has just been put up just E. of point 54.
WIRE observed between enemy 2nd and 3rd lines at about 57.
Old chevaux de frise, much knocked about but re-wired to some extent from point 59 to Barricade just N. of point 60, thence to 56 salient low wire entanglement, very closely interwoven-brown-(rusty?)-15 to 20 feet deep-a very formidable obstacle.
Low wire entanglement along 2nd line trench in S 11 b to point 51 - again between points 54 and 56. It is expected also between 51 and 54, covered by low earth banks, but this needs confirmation.

Major R.A.
Brigade Major, Royal Artillery,
MEERUT DIVISION

"A" Form. APPENDIX 14b(2) Army Form C. 2121.
MESSAGES AND SIGNALS. No. of Message

Prefix SB Code FCP Words 52

Office of Origin and Service Instructions: Y1G

Recd. at 6.25 p.m.

TO C R A

Sender's Number: G 403/30 Day of Month: 24   AAA

Indian Corps wires begins G761 24th relief of portion of Meerut Divn by troops of 4th Corps cancelled for the present ends for information addressed BAREILLY BDE CRA MEERUT repeated 4th DIVN GARHWAL DEHRADUN BDES CRE MEERUT MEERUT SIGS and Meerut Train

From: MEERUT DIVN
Time: 4 (Z)

"A" Form.   Army Form C. 2121.
MESSAGES AND SIGNALS.   No. of Message

APPENDIX 146(1)

Prefix	Code	m.	Words	Charge	This message is on a/c of:	Recd. at	m.
Office of Origin and Service Instructions			Sent			Date	
			At	m.	Service.	From	
			To			By	
			By		(Signature of "Franking Officer.")		

TO	O.C. 43rd Bde RFA

Sender's Number.	Day of Month.	In reply to Number	AAA
736 RA(L)	24		

Meerut Divn wires begin @ 12/1 24 Indian Corps wires begin @ 7.56 24th following units will join LAHORE Divn tomorrow AAA 43rd How Bde RFA less one Bty AAA Howitzer will be taken out of line tonight and proceed by LA GORGUE NEUF BERQUIN BLEU METEREN to BOESCHAEPE AAA Report hour at which Bde will reach LA GORGUE ends AAA March should be so timed that Bde will not pass through LESTREM before 8 a.m AAA Send Officer of 43rd Bde to report to LAHORE Divn GODEWAERS -VELDE tomorrow ahead of Unit AAA ends AAA Report time at which Bde

From
Place
Time

The above may be forwarded as now corrected.   (Z)

Censor.   Signature of Addressee or person authorised to telegraph in his name.
* This line should be erased if not required.

"A" Form.   Army Form C. 2121.

MESSAGES AND SIGNALS.   No. of Message_____

Prefix___ Code___ m.	Words	Charge	This message is on a/c of:	Recd. at_____ m.
Office of Origin and Service Instructions	Sent		_____ Service.	Date_____
	At_____ m.			From_____
	To			
	By		(Signature of "Franking Officer.")	By_____

TO ●

| Sender's Number. | Day of Month. | In reply to Number. | AAA |

will	read	LA	GORGUE	please
AAA	Officer	i/c	your	section
of	Div	A.C.	has	been
ordered	to	report	to	you
for	orders	AAA	Possibly	it
would	be	best	if	he
were	to	join	it	will
your	Bde	A.C.	en	route
AAA	Please	issue	necessary	orders
to	him	AAA	Report	action
taken				

From BMRA Meerut
Place
Time 4-45 p.m.

The above may be forwarded as now corrected.   (Z) _____

Censor.   Signature of Addresser or person authorised to telegraph in his name.
* This line should be erased if not required.

"A" Form.   Army Form C. 2121.

MESSAGES AND SIGNALS.

APPENDIX 146(?)

TO: O.C. 13th Bty RA Southern Group

Sender's Number: 733 RA(L)
Day of Month: 24
AAA

Two sections of 30th How Bty are grouped with O.C. RA Centre Section for defence of DEHRA DUN front AAA All registration of this zone together with telephone line to O.P. should be taken over by 30th Bty from 40th Bty before latter moves AAA If necessary 4 guns of 30th must be

MESSAGES AND SIGNALS.

move into position of 40⁵
Bty after dark tonight
AAA Remaining @ section
remains grouped with you
for defence of GARHWAL
front AAA Inform
30? Bty accordingly AAA
If possible even tho from present
position the two sections need
not move but registration of new

"A" Form.
MESSAGES AND SIGNALS.
Army Form C. 2121.

Zero on DEHRA DUN front should be carried out forthwith AAA For information and necessary action please

From BMRA
Time 3.27 pm

APPENDIX 147

SECRET

TACTICAL PROGRESS REPORT
25th April 1915.

1(a) ACTION BY OUR OWN ARTILLERY
11.a.m. 68th Battery fired on point 63.
11.30.a.m. 20th Battery fired 6 rounds at houses near point 259.
11.45.a.m. 7th Battery fired at party of men observed in communicating trench near point 65.
3.p.m. 8th Battery registered enemy trench between S 10 b 4'1 and S 10 b 9'4.
3.30.p.m. 24th Heavy Battery fired at points 63, 69, "L" shaped farm, 124, 123 and 120, observation by Observing Officer of 68th Battery.
3.35.p.m. 19th Battery registered on "Machine Gun" house in M 36 d 7'8 and at 4.p.m. fired 10 H.E. shell at it, obtaining 7 direct hits.
4.p.m. 14th Battery registered house M 36 d 8'7.
14th Battery obtained 2 direct hits on house at point 122 during registration
30th How: Battery registered points in its newly allotted zone.
5th Siege Battery registered points 50 and 51 and houses N.W.
LA TOURELLE during the day by visual observation, and FERME du BIEZ by aeroplane observation

1(b) ACTION BY HOSTILE ARTILLERY
12 noon to 2.p.m. Enemy shelled BREWERY in NEUVE CHAPELLE and neighbourhood with 10'5 c.m. from Ht POMMEREAU.
3.30.p.m. PIPSQUEAK shelled vicinity M 24 c 8'9 at long intervals.
4.p.m. Several H.E. shell fired at M 23 d 3'3.
4.15.p.m. PIPSQUEAK shelled area between the MIN and M 15 b.
15 c.m. Howitzer shelled the RITZ four times during the day, without however obtaining a direct hit.

2. INFORMATION
BOMBING during night 24th/25th - A good deal of "Bombing".
between 6.30.p.m. and 9.30.p.m. from points 141, S 36 c 9'9 and 263(SNIPER's HOUSE).
6.p.m. Bomb guns again active from point 263- 2nd Battery replied.
SNIPING "GOOD LUCK" House heavily sniped during afternoon.
MINING Infantry report enemy using electric drill on night 24th/25th near points 257 and 262.
MACHINE GUN reported at M 36 d 7'8(DOIL's HOUSE).
LISTENING POST located in small sap near point 268.
WORK:- A new parapet has been made between point 253 and point 255, higher than the German front trench parapet. There are new revetments between points 253 and 257, and between 252 and 259.
Germans seen carrying planks for this work.
There is much hammering and work at point 257 at night time.
A Parados revetted with boards is being constructed in M 30 a and M 30 c.
OBSTACLES:- Chevaux de Frise opposite point 263.
New wire appears to have been put up in front of barricade on LA BASSEE Road.
HOSTILE AIRCRAFT:- None were seen.

7.a.m. 26.4.15.- Quiet night. Infantry strongly suspect mining from point 257.

Major R.A.

Brigade Major, Royal Artillery,
MEERUT DIVISION.

"A" Form.   Army Form C. 2121.

MESSAGES AND SIGNALS.   No. of Message _____

Prefix	Code	m.	Words	Charge	APPENDIX 147(a)	Recd. at _____ m.
Office of Origin and Service Instructions					This message is on a/c of:	Date _____
			Sent		_____ Service.	From _____
			At _____ m.			
			To		(Signature of "Franking Officer.")	By _____
			By			

TO	O.C. No 4 Trench Howitzer Btty

Sender's Number.	Day of Month.	In reply to Number	
749 RA(L)	25		AAA

Under	orders	received	from	Meerut
Divn	your	battery	is	placed
at	disposal	of	Bareilly	Bde
for	work	tonight	and	tomorrow
night	AAA	You	should	report
to	Bareilly	Bde	Hd Qrs	
M.14.b.	10.0	early	to-day	AAA
On	return	report	to	staff
Captain	RA	for	orders	here.

From: BMRA Meerut
Place:
Time: 9.4.n

The above may be forwarded as now corrected.   (Z)   [signature]
                                                 Censor.   Signature of Addressor or person authorised to telegraph in his name.

* This line should be erased if not required.

SECRET   MEERUT DIVISIONAL ARTILLERY   APPENDIX 147(2) 25/4/1915.

Headquarters G.O.C., R.A.,..........................FOSSE R 21 b 2'8.

GROUPS

"Northern Group" for support of BAREILLY Brigade.

R.A. Group Commander Lt Colonel F. POTTS...Headquarters R 24 a 7'9.
    28th Battery R.F.A. 9th Brigade R.F.A.,,,,M 15 b 5 3.
    20th Battery R.F.A. 9th Brigade R.F.A.....M 21 b 6 7.
    19th Battery R.F.A. 9th Brigade R.F.A.,,,,M 21 a 3 3.
    2nd Battery R.F.A.13th Brigade R.F.A.....M 33 a 9 9.
    30th How: Battery R.F.A.(4 guns).........M 32 a 2 5.

"Centre Group" for support of DEHRA DUN Brigade.

R.A. Group Commander Colonel L.A.C. GORDON, Headquarters M 26 c 5' 2.
    14th Battery R.F.A. 4th Brigade R.F.A.....M 20 c 9 1.
    7th Battery R.F.A. 4th Brigade R.F.A.....M 26 c 7 5.
    66th Battery R.F.A. 4th Brigade R.F.A.....M 33 a 2 2.
    44th Battery R.F.A.13th Brigade R.F.A.....M 31 d 4 9.
    30th How: Battery R.F.A.(2 guns).........M 32 b 5 7.

"Southern Group" for support of GARHWAL Brigade.

R.A. Group Commander Lt Colonel J.A. TYLER, Headquarters M 29 c 3'1.
    8th Battery R.F.A. 13th Brigade R.F.A....M 31 b 8 7.

DIVISIONAL ARTILLERY

    6th Brigade R.G.A.(Less 1 battery).
O.C. Lt Colonel EYRE.........................Headquarters R 27 d.
    2nd Siege Battery R.G.A..............M 32 c XN 10 2.
    5th Siege Battery R.G.A.,,..........M 31 b 6 2.

Note:-   The above two batteries are retained under the control of the G.O.C., R.A., but arrange "Night lines" to cover front of "Centre" and "Southern" Groups, and are available in case of emergency- these two groups lacking howitzers.

1st Section Anti Aircraft at M 32 a 3.7
1 Section 5th Mountain Btty (billets) R 10 d
No 4 Trench Mortar Btty   billets   "

                                        Major R.A.

Copy No...3....   for Commanding Royal Artillery,
                                   MEERUT DIVISION.

SECRET
APPENDIX 148

TACTICAL PROGRESS REPORT
28th April 1915.

1(a) ACTION BY OUR OWN ARTILLERY

9.a.m. 2nd Siege Battery registered Barricade 48.
11.a.m. 8th Battery carried on registration on hostile trenches and communication trench V.8. latter with object of catching reliefs coming up in evening.
11.20.a.m. 7th Battery fired on house 30 yards S.W. of 125, snipers being active from there.
11.30.a.m. 14th Battery fired on houses 173 and 184. Infantry co-operated with rifle fire.
1.30.p.m. 20th Battery fired 4 rounds on AUBERS Ridge.
12.5.p.m. 66th Battery fired on sandbag emplacement near 130.
12.45.p.m. 66th Battery fired on house 66 and on trench in front of it.
2.30.p.m. 66th Battery fired on house 80.
3.5.p.m. 7th Battery fired on enemy O.P. point 85 - 3 hits on house.
3.30.p.m. 2nd Siege Battery registered house on LA BASSEE Road S 11 c 2'8.
3.40.p.m. 66th Battery fired on Barricade at point 133.
4.p.m. 20th Battery fired 4 rounds on house in N 31 d 5'2.
4.45.p.m. 26th Battery fired 4 rounds on machine gun emplacement at MIN du PIETRE.
6.20.p.m. 7th Battery fired a few rounds to stop heavy rifle fire on our aeroplane which was flying very low down.
6.15 to 7.p.m. 66th Battery shelled enemy trenches in reply to shelling of NEUVE CHAPELLE.

1(b) ACTION BY HOSTILE ARTILLERY

3.p.m. "PIPSQUEAK" fired 15 rounds from N.E. of BOIS du BIEZ into vicinity M 27 d, obtaining 4 direct hits on house at M 27 d 6'8.
5.30.p.m. "PIPSQUEAK" shelled house near cross road at M 33 b 5'7.
6.15 to 7.p.m. Enemy shelled NEUVE CHAPELLE and our support trenches at M 29 c 2'6 with 21 c.m. Howitzers from near HERLIES.
7.p.m. Enemy shelled locality of our "bomb" gun opposite point 202 and road at M 35 a 7'5.

2. INFORMATION

MACHINE GUN:- A machine gun is believed to be at MIN du PIETRE.
BOMBING:- Large bombs reported falling near FAUQUISSART at 6.15.p.m. Two heavy bombs fell at M 29 c 2'6 at 6.45.p.m. and "F" Sub-section was heavily bombed at the same time from point 204.
WORK:- Enemy appears to have been strengthening their parapet from S 10 d 5'6 to S 10 d 3'7.
There is a deep ditch in front of parapet of trench which runs across N.W. corner of S 11 b. This requires confirmation, as from the PICQUET House it is not easy to distinguish this trench from that running past 45 and 46; latter probably not visible from PICQUET House.
WIRE:- There is low wire entanglement between points 55 and 57. Many iron posts appear to be in the entanglement from point 55 to V.8.
MINING expected near point 257.
HOSTILE AIRCRAFT:- None were seen to-day.

7.a.m. 27th April 1915. During night 26/27 our patrols reported 4 enemy field guns behind point 203, and enemy reported felling large trees in small wood near there, possibly to improve field of fire for these guns.
18th Battery employed "searching" .... AUBERS Ridge during night.

Brigade Major, Royal Artillery,
MEERUT DIVISION

APPENDIX 148(a)

Copy No. 1

OPERATION ORDER No. 28.
by
LIEUT:-GENERAL Sir C.A. ANDERSON, K.C.B.,
Commanding MEERUT Division.

Reference map:-
BOIS du BIEZ 1:10,000 &
Map of France 1:40,000.   26th April 1915.

Information   1.   Under instructions from 1st Army the 4th Corps is
                      taking over the front of the Indian Corps as far south as
                      the road 121-140-142 exclusive.

RELIEFS.   2.   The following reliefs will take place on the nights
                      27th/28th, 28th/29th and 29th/30th April:-
Bareilly Bde   (a)   20th Inf. Bde. relieves Bareilly Bde in front
                            line Northern Section.
Garhwal Bde   (b)   Garhwal Bde relieves Dehra Dun Bde in Centre
                            Section.
Dehra Dun Bde   (c)   Dehra Dun Bde relieves Garhwal Bde in Southern
                            Section.
                      Details connected with the reliefs will be arranged
                      direct between Brigade Commanders concerned.
                      Brigade Commanders will hand over command of their
                      Sections as the relief of their troops is completed.
                      Movements will be made in accordance with the attached
                      March Table.

Divisional   3.   Bareilly Bde will be in Divisional Reserve.
Reserve.

Artillery   4.   Artillery reliefs will be carried out under arrange-
                      ments to be made direct by G.O.C., R.A., Meerut and 7th
                      Divisions.

Machine guns   5.   The Machine Gun Detachment, 4th Ind. Cavalry will
4th Ind.Cav.   rejoin its unit on night 27th/28th April.

Area.   6.   The new billeting area will be as shown by the
                      tracing issued with Operation Order 27.

                                                General Staff,
                                                MEERUT DIVISION.

Issued to Signal Company
at 12 midnight 26th/27th
for delivery:-
Copy No. 1   to   Indian Corps
        2   7th Division   12   Divnl Train
        3   1st Division   13   A.A. & Q.M.G.
        4   Dehra Dun Bde   14   D.A.A.G.
        5   Garhwal Bde   15   D.A.A. & Q.M.G.
        6   Bareilly Bde   16   A.D.M.S.
        7   Divnl Arty.   17
        8   Divnl Engrs   18
        9   4th Ind.Cav.   19   War Diary & files.
       10   107th Pioneers   20
       11   Meerut Signals   21

MARCH TABLE.
(To accompany Meerut Division Operation Order No 28)

Date.	Unit.	From.	To.	Route.	Remarks.
1.	2.	3.	4.	5.	6.
April 27th/28th.	2 Battalions BAREILLY BDE.	"G" & "H" Subsections.	Area VIEILLE CHAPELLE LESLOBES, LE TOMBE VILLOT.	ROUGE CROIX, HARROW Rd WELLINGTON ROAD.	On relief by 20th Brigade.
do.	2 Battalions GARHWAL BDE.	VIEILLE CHAPELLE & LA COUTURE.	Trenches CENTRE SECTION.	LACOUTURE, CROIX BARBEE OXFORD ROAD, LORETTO. RD.	In relief of two bns. Dehra Dun Brigade.
do.	2 battalions DEHRA DUN BDE.	Trenches "C" & "D" Subsections, Centre Section.	VIEILLE CHAPELLE & LA COUTURE.	LORETTO Road, OXFORD Road, CROIX BARBEE, LACOUTURE.	On relief by Garhwal Brigade.
April 28th/29th.	2 battalions BAREILLY BDE.	Trenches "E" & "F" Subsections.	Area LESLOBES LE TOMBE VILLOT.	ROUGE CROIX, HARROW Road WELLINGTON Road.	On relief by 20th Bde. Balance of Brigade to march to new billeting area under orders of G.O.C. Bareilly Brigade.
do.	1 battalion DEHRA DUN BDE.	From billets.	Trenches SOUTHERN SECTION.	CROIX BARBEE, ST VAAST Road Junction.	In relief of Garhwal Brigade.
do.	1 battalion GARHWAL BDE.	Trenches SOUTHERN SECT.	Billets VIEILLE CHAPELLE, LA COUTURE.	ST VAAST Road Junction, CROIX BARBEE	On relief by Dehra Dun Brigade.
April 29th/30th.	2 battalions GARHWAL BDE.	VIEILLE CHAPELLE & LA COUTURE.	Trenches "A" & "B" Subsections.	CROIX BARBEE, LORETTO Road.	In relief of 2 battalions Dehra Dun Brigade.
do.	2 battalions DEHRA DUN BDE.	Trenches "A" & "B" Subsection.	VIEILLE CHAPELLE and LA COUTURE.	LORETTO Road & CROIX BARBEE.	Remainder of Brigade to march to new billets under orders of G.O.C. Brigade.

G-406/49.

Head Quarters, MEERUT Division.

April 27th 1915.

Memorandum.

Reference MEERUT Division Operation Order No.28, para 2 lines 11 and 12.

G.O.C. MEERUT Division and G.O.C. BAREILLY BRIGADE will hand over command of the Northern Section to the G.O.C. 7th Division and G.O.C. 20th Brigade respectively at 10 p.m. on 28th April 1915.

                     Croni   Colonel,
            General Staff, MEERUT Division.

To,
    Indian Corps.
    7th Division.
    Dehra Dun Brigade.
    Garhwal Brigade.
    Bareilly Brigade.
    C.R.A.
    C.R.E.
    107th Pioneers.
    Signal Company.
Copy for information,
    "Q.A"
    "Q".
    "A".
    A.D.M.S.

SECRET   APPENDIX 149

TACTICAL PROGRESS REPORT
27th April 1915.

1(a) ACTION BY OUR OWN ARTILLERY
12 midnight 26th/27th 28th Battery fired 6 rounds on points 257 and 263 at request of Infantry.
12.15.a.m. 19th Battery opened searching fire for guns located in wood behind point 202, where enemy were reported felling trees (also at 10.30.p.m. on 26th April 1915).
1.a.m. 28th Battery again fired 6 rounds at points 257 and 263.
2nd Siege Battery registered in early morning on point 125 and cross roads 63.
11.a.m. 2nd Battery registered on machine gun emplacement 20 yards N.E. of 140.
12.10.p.m. 66th Battery registered point 62.
12.15.p.m. 2nd Battery replied to bombing of our "listening post", which took place from rear of trench at point 140.
12.30.p.m. 14th Battery fired 3 rounds at house 100 yards S. of 151.
1.10.p.m. 2nd Battery replied to further "bombing" at our "listening post" and house in M 36 d 4.7, obtaining direct hits on parapet.
4.p.m. 14th Battery fired at house at cross roads near 125.
4.20.p.m. 7th Battery fired a few rounds at snipers in hostile trenches.
4.30.p.m. 30th How: Battery registered trenches at 137 and 126.
5.45.p.m. 66th Battery fired on point 62.

1(b) ACTION BY HOSTILE ARTILLERY
1.p.m. 3 shell fell near road junction M 36 a.
1.10.p.m. "PIPSQUEAK" shelled our trenches in "B" sub-section.
1.15.p.m. M 34 b 3.4 had 6 77 m.m. shell fired at it from S.E.
1.10.p.m. 10.5 c.m. How: shelled NEUVE CHAPELLE from direction M 31 a.
1.20.p.m. 15 c.m. How: shelled ROUGE CROIX and vicinity M 22 c from the direction of HAUTE POMMEREAU.
1.50.p.m. Enemy 10 c.m. gun shelled reserve trenches in rear of NEUVE CHAPELLE.
2.20 and 2.35.p.m. flashes of 10.5 c.m. How: observed from M1N(M 22 d 2.4) 141° magnetic.
3.p.m. Heavy fire heard from near FAUQUISSART.
A hostile battery is reported to be near point 119 at Northern end of BOIS du BIEZ.

2. INFORMATION
WORKING PARTY of 30 Germans visible up to their waists, working on trench between 48 and 49 in early morning. They knocked off at 8.a.m.
Germans working in the trenches opposite point 26, men were using heavy sledge hammers for driving spikes where.
HOSE PIPES located at:-
(i) Between points 59 and 7.6 (about half way). The rear end of this rests on a V shaped board- this suggests it is near the pumping.
(ii) A few yards visible running N.E. from point 67.
These lengths of pipe appear to be the ordinary armoured rubber piping.
(iii) A large pipe seen over parapet at 120, two others 50 yards apart near point 86.

                                                            Major R.A.
                                            Brigade Major, Royal Artillery,
                                                    MEERUT DIVISION.

SECRET   OPERATION ORDER No. 17.   Copy No 14
                          by
       Brigadier General R.St.C. LECKY, R.A., C.R.A. MEERUT Division

Reference:-   APPENDIX 150
Map-FRANCE 1/40,000.   27th April 1915.

INFORMATION   1. Under instructions from 1st Army the 4th Corps is taking over
                 the front of the INDIAN Corps as far as the road 121-149-142
                 inclusive.
RELIEFS   2. The following reliefs are taking place on the nights 27th/
                 28th, 28th/29th, 29th/30th April:-
  BAREILLY   (a) 20th Infantry Brigade relieves BAREILLY Brigade in the
  Brigade.   front line Northern Section as follows:-
                     (i) "G" & "H" Sub-sections on night 27th/28th.
                     (ii) "E" & "F" Sub-sections on night 28th/29th.
  GARHWAL   (b) GARHWAL Brigade relieves DEHRA DUN Brigade in Centre
  Brigade.   Section as follows:-
                     (i) "C" & "D" Sub-sections on night 27th/28th.
                     (ii) "A" & "B" Sub-sections on night 29th/30th.
  DEHRA DUN   (c) DEHRA DUN Brigade relieves GARHWAL Brigade in Southern
  Brigade.   Section on night 28th/29th.
                 Details connected with these reliefs are being arranged
                 between Infantry Brigadiers, and R.A. Group Commanders should
                 make themselves acquainted with such as concern them.
DIVISIONAL   3. BAREILLY Brigade will be in Divisional Reserve.
RESERVE.
ARTILLERY   4. The Artillery of the MEERUT Division with 30th How: Battery
                 and 6th Brigade R.G.A. (less one battery) will remain in action
                 for the defence of the INDIAN Corps front.
ARTILLERY   5. Artillery reliefs will be carried out as follows:-
RELIEFS   19th and 20th Batteries will be relieved by 2 Batteries West
                 Riding Field Artillery on nights 27th/28th and 28th/29th, in
                 accordance with instructions already issued.
See attached   (2nd, 28th, 30th How: (less 1 section) Batteries will be with-
List of positions drawn on night 29th/30th and will proceed to positions which
                 will be notified later.
                 O.C. 9th Brigade R.F.A. will retain command of all the
                 Artillery mentioned above for the support of the Infantry of
                 "E", "F", "G" & "H" Sub-sections until 10.a.m. on 29th, when he
                 will hand over command to O.C. 33rd Brigade R.F.A. Hd Qrs-
                 PARADIS; He will maintain communication with G.O.C., 20th
                 Infantry Brigade from the time the latter takes over command
                 from G.O.C. BAREILLY Brigade until 10.a.m. 29th.
ARTILLERY   6. The present R.A. Centre Group will continue to support the
GROUPS.   Infantry holding "A", "B", "C" & "D" Sub-sections, and the
                 present Southern Group will continue to support the Infantry
                 holding the Southern Section.
AMMUNITION   7. 9th Brigade R.F.A. will continue to supply S.A.A. to BAREILLY
                 Brigade.
                 4th Brigade R.F.A. will continue to supply S.A.A. to the
                 Infantry holding "A", "B", "C" & "D" Sub-sections.
                 13th Brigade R.F.A. will continue to supply S.A.A. to Infantry
                 holding Southern Section.
                 Officers Commanding Brigade Ammunition Columns will report to
                 Staff Captains of Infantry Brigades for orders.
COMMAND   8. The G.O.C., R.A., MEERUT Division will remain in command of
                 the Artillery supporting present front until 10.a.m. on 29th
                 April 1915, when G.O.C., R.A., 8th Division assumes command of
                 the Artillery supporting "E", "F", "G" & "H" Sub-sections.
REPORTS   9. Headquarters MEERUT Divisional Artillery will remain at FOSSE.
                 Headquarters 8th Divisional Artillery will remain at SAILLY.

Issued at 3.30.p.m.   Major R.A.
by motor cyclist.   Brigade Major, Royal Artillery,
                                              MEERUT DIVISION.

Copy No. 1 to General Staff, MEERUT Division.
Copy No. 2 to General Staff, 8th Division.   Copy No 9 to O.C.R.A. Northern Gp
Copy No. 3 to General Staff, 7th Division.   Copy No.10 to O.C.R.A. Centre Group
Copy No. 4 to G.O.C., R.A., 8th Division.   Copy No.11 to O.C.R.A. Southern Gp
Copy No. 5 to 20th Infantry Brigade.   Copy No.12 to O.C. 6th Bde R.G.A.
Copy No. 6 to BAREILLY Brigade.   Copy No.13 to O.C. MEERUT D.A.C.
Copy No. 7 to GARHWAL Brigade.   Copy No.14 to War Diary.
Copy No. 8 to DEHRA DUN Brigade.   Copy No.15 to File.

Attached to APPENDIX 150

SECRET   Copy....

INSTRUCTIONS FOR MOVES OF SOUTHERN GROUP, MEERUT
DIVISIONAL ARTILLERY 29th APRIL 1915.

(1) 2nd Battery R.F.A. M 33 a 9'8 will march at 9.30.p.m. and will be all clear of its position by 9.45.p.m. moving to new position M 32 a 4'6 via CROIX BARBEE.

(2) 9th Battery R.F.A. M 15 b will march at 9.30.p.m. via PONT du HEM, ROUGE CROIX and road junction M 27 d to M 33 a 9'8.

(3) 20th How: Battery R.F.A.(2 sections) M 22 a 0'2 will march at 9.30.p.m. via PONT du HEM, road junction M 21 a, road junction M 26 a and CROIX BARBEE to M 32 d 4'4.

(4) All vehicles must be clear of roads by 10.30.p.m. on account of Infantry reliefs.

Major R.A.

for Commanding Royal Artillery,
MEERUT DIVISION.

G.S., MEERUT Division..........Copy No.1.
O.C. R.A. Northern Group......Copy No.2.
O.C. R.A. Centre Group........Copy No.3.
O.C. R.A. Southern Group......Copy No.4.
O.C. 20th How:Battery R.F.A.Copy No.5.
G.O.C., R.A. 8th Division.....Copy No.6.

"A" Form. **APPENDIX 130(a)** Army Form C. 2121.
MESSAGES AND SIGNALS.
No. of Message

Prefix S15 Code ACP m. | Words 43 | Charge | This message is on a/c of: | Recd. at 1.25 P m.
Office of Origin and Service Instructions. VIG | Sent At ...m. To... By... | ...Service. (Signature of "Franking Officer.") | Date 28/4/15. From VIG By HW Gray Cpl.
Priority

TO CRA Meerut

Sender's Number G411/4 | Day of Month 25th | In reply to Number | AAA

1st Army orders that all hose pipes which are seen protruding over enemy trenches should be destroyed by arty fire forthwith and report of action taken and results forwarded immediately aaa For action please

From Meerut
Place
Time 1.15 pm

APPENDIX 151

SECRET

TACTICAL PROGRESS REPORT
28th April 1915.

1(a) ACTION BY OUR OWN ARTILLERY.
 8.45.a.m. 4th Brigade Batteries shelled enemy trench near pt 140 in retaliation for Germans shelling NEUVE CHAPELLE at 8.42.a.m.
 10.a.m. Section of 30th How:Battery fired at point 130.
 10.45.a.m. 66th Battery fired on point 130.
 11.20.a.m. 66th Battery fired at trench near point 63.
 11.30.a.m. 28th Battery fired 4 rounds at SNIPER's HOUSE(263) and 3 rounds at point 260 by request of Infantry.
 11.50.a.m. 2nd Battery fired 4 rds at N.W. corner of BOIS du BIEZ.
 2.p.m. 5th Siege Battery registered LA TOURELLE cross roads.
 2.45.p.m. 28th Battery fired on "Hose Pipe" visible about 50 yds E. of 257 with H.E. and shrapnel; 3 direct hits were obtained with shrapnel, a good deal of parapet demolished and hose pipe disappeared.
 3.p.m. 8th Battery fired 8 shrapnel and 3 H.E. at "Hose Pipe" in S 10 b 5.4-5 direct hits on parapet, to which considerable damage was done-Detonation of 1 H.E. behind parapet threw up large column of water.
 3.45.p.m. 14th Battery fired at house 100 yards S.W. of pt 151. There is a haystack close to the house, which obviously has a 'dug-out' underneath it.
 6.5.p.m. 66th Battery fired on Hose Pipe at point 131 and destroyed it.
 6.15.p.m. 7th Battery fired 16 rounds on two hose pipes near point 68. Direct hits obtained on parapets at both points.
 6.45.p.m. 44th Battery fired 25 rounds on Hose Pipe near point 57. Several rounds hit parapet close by, and hose pipes are considered to have been destroyed.
 7.p.m. 2nd Battery fired a few rounds at enemy trenches to check hostile rifle fire on our aeroplanes, with desired result.

1(b) ACTION BY HOSTILE ARTILLERY
 Enemy batteries fairly active throughout the day.
 8.40.a.m. Enemy shelled support trenches behind NEUVE CHAPELLE with H.E. and shrapnel, from direction of HAUTE POMMEREAU.
 9.30.a.m., 11.a.m. to 11.15.a.m. & 12.30.p.m. "PIPSQUEAK" active on Gurkha Headquarters from N.E. corner of BOIS du BIEZ
 9.55.a.m. PIPSQUEAK fired 3 rounds on "E" Sub-section support trenches, from direction of AUBERS.
 10.20.a.m. German 10'5.c.m. How: shelled the vicinity of M 23 d 4'3.
 10.25.a.m. Same battery shelled road junction M 22 c 3'5 from direction of HAUTE POMMEREAU.
 1.30.p.m. WINDY CORNER shelled by 15.c.m.
 2.p.m. 10'5.c.m. fired a few rds in vicinity of M 32 d 8'2.
 2.15.p.m. Several 10'5.c.m. shell dropped in neighbourhood of S 3 c 5'8.
 4.p.m. 77.m.m. gun retaliated on our trenches for our bombardment of their hose pipes.
 4.30.p.m. Same battery(Field)fired several rounds of gun fire on CHAPIGNY, followed by fire from 10'5.c.m. Howitzer.
 6.40.p.m. PORT ARTHUR shelled by Howitzers.
 7.15 to 7.45.p.m. PIPSQUEAK dropped shell in square R 34 b 3'5 - all were blind except two bursts in air.

2. INFORMATION
 TELEGRAPH WIRES:- 8th Battery F.O.O. reported at 9.30.a.m. that several telegraph wires visible in trench S 11 c 4'2. They seemed to lead into a house close in rear. New wooden beams were also noticeable here.
 TRAFFIC:- Considerable noise from wheeled traffic reported again behind enemy's lines from direction of PIETRE cross roads last night.
 WORKS:- New work observed at S 10 d 6'10 running S.W. for 80 yards.
 OBSTACLES:- Iron spikes noticed on top of barricade near pt 60.
 New wire appears to be in course of laying at this spot, some coils visible Entanglements opposite our "Advanced Post"(196)appear to have been strengthened. There is a wire on high angle-iron posts behind chevaux-de-frise from pt 204 to 146. High wire entanglement runs across the road about 150 yds W. of pt 259. There is new high wire entanglement behind the enemy's first line trench, from pt 256 to pt 262.

P.T.O.

PHOTOGRAPHS:- A HUN was observed taking photographs - PORT ARTHUR over the parapet between points 56 and 30.
FUZE:- One fuze marked "R. STOCK & Co." was picked up.
MACHINE GUNS:- A machine gun emplacement was located 100 yds N. of pt 263.
SNIPING:- Our Infantry complain that they are much bothered by sniping from houses at point 263 and 260 and express a desire for the destruction of these houses.
BOMBING:- "SWAN NECK" trench M 36 a bombed at 11.25.a.m. in reply to bombing of their trench by "Trench Mortar".
HOSTILE AIRCRAFT:- 8.45.a.m. AVIATIK sighted flying high, bearing 115°, engaged 8 rounds by ARCHIBALD and turned S.E.
10.15.a.m. AVIATIK sighted high, bearing 115°, engaged 43 rounds, turned E. and disappeared. Re-appeared and again engaged with 27 rounds, F.M.E. out of range.
10.25.a.m. FOKKER seen high, bearing 75°, engaged 2 rounds, turned E, out of range.

MORNING REPORT 29th APRIL 1915

Enemy trench mortar active between 3.10.a.m. and 4.30.a.m., especially between PIQUET House and RITZ. The 8th Battery fired a few rounds at 4.a.m. to stop this.
Heavy firing heard to the North about 4.a.m.

Major F.A.

SECRET

APPENDIX 152

TACTICAL PROGRESS REPORT
29th April, 1916
****

1(a). ACTION BY OUR OWN ARTILLERY
4.30.a.m. 8th Battery fired on German trench in front of ORCHARD Redoubt at request of Infantry in order to stop "Bombing". This was achieved.
7.a.m. 2nd Siege Battery registered LIGNY le GRAND with aeroplane.
11.10.p.m. 86th Battery fired a few rounds on houses near 65 and 66- The latter was set on fire.
11.35.a.m. 7th Battery fired on House 63 reported by Infantry to contain machine guns.
12.30.p.m. 44th Battery fired on working party at 66.
12.30.p.m. 8th Battery registered on point near N.E. from which hostile "Bombing" takes place.
4.30.p.m. 14th Battery fired on house 100 yards N.E. of point 151 with haystack and "dug-out" on its right.
4.45.p.m. 84th Battery fired 6 rounds at snipers in house near 85.
5.15.p.m. 30th How: Battery(1 section)fired on Redoubt just N. of 63.
6.30.p.m. 30th How: Battery(1 section)registered road junction 125.
In the evening 20th Battery registered certain points in their new zone by aeroplane.

1(b) ACTION BY HOSTILE ARTILLERY
6.a.m. German 10.5 c.m. Howitzer fired about 20 rounds at house at cross roads M 35 c 2 3, obtaining 3 direct hits.
7.15 to 7.40.a.m. PORT ARTHUR shelled by 15 c.m.
7.20.a.m. Support trenches of "F" Sub-section shelled with H.E. and shrapnel from direction of HAUTE POMMEREAU.
10.50.a.m. 10.5 c.m. Howitzer shelled house at cross roads at M 16 c 2 5 from direction of HAUTE POMMEREAU.
12 noon. 10'5 c.m. Howitzer shelled "RITZ" hitting it 2 or 3 times.
1.p.m. and 1.35.p.m. PIPSQUEAK shelled vicinity of 44th Battery O.P.- GOOD LUCK House.
2.p.m. 3 rounds 15 c.m. fell near PORT ARTHUR.
3.30.p.m. PIPSQUEAK fired on party proceeding along RUE du PUITS and RUE du RACQUEROT.
3.45.p.m. Same battery fired on reserve trenches in M 22 a.
4.30 p.m. Same battery did good shooting at Haystack in front of M1A L. M 28 d 7'7" and then turned on to PONT du HEM.
7th Battery O.P. shelled 5 times during the day-several direct hits.

2. INFORMATION
INFANTRY:- 4.a.m. Enemy "Bombed" ORCHARD Redoubt, but were stopped by fire of 8th Battery.
11.30.a.m. to 12.30.p.m. intermittent "Bombing" in neighbourhood of "ORCHARD".

AIRCRAFT:- 9.10.a.m. ALBATROSS sighted flying high, bearing 90°, out of range, turned S.E. over German lines.
9.12.a.m. AVIATIK flying high, bearing 40°,engaged with 72 rounds, turned N.N.E. over German lines, reappeared at bearing 40°,engaged with 30 rounds, turned S. over German lines, not observed.
The 2nd Battery assisted in this "shoot", fire-direct observation by telephone.

BALLOONS:- Following were observed at 9.30 a.m.:-
1 Sausage Balloon bearing 170° magnetic. 1 Spherical Balloon bearing 1   "   "   "   "   "   2310

In all cases from POINT du HEM.

                                                                     Major R.A.
                                                              Brigade Major, Royal Artillery
                                                              MEERUT DIVISION

SECRET.

APPENDIX 15

TACTICAL PROGRESS REPORT
30th April 1915.

1(a) ACTION BY OUR OWN ARTILLERY

9.10.a.m. 6th Battery fired 2 shrapnel at Machine Gun at point 59 at request of O.C. 6th Jats.
10.5.a.m. 66th Battery fired at house at point 65.
11.25.a.m. 7th Battery fired a few rounds at snipers near point 131 which had been annoying our Infantry.
11.35.a.m. 66th Battery fired at point 65 (O.P.).
12.15.p.m. 66th Battery fired on "L" shaped house near point 125.
3.p.m. 8th Battery fired shrapnel and H.E. at Machine Gun at point 59. Fire was effective, parapet where Machine Gun was located being breached.
6.p.m. 14th Battery fired on trenches at 145 and 66th Battery at trenches 130-131 to keep down rifle fire on our aeroplane.
6.5.p.m. 2nd Siege Battery registered LORGIES with aeroplane.
6.50.p.m. 14th Battery fired at likely O.P. at M 36 d 5.8.
5th Siege Battery registered point in enemy trenches at S.11 a 9.4, which appeared mid-way between points 53 and 54.
30th How. Battery carried out registration.

1(b) ACTION BY HOSTILE ARTILLERY

11.40.a.m. Heavy Howitzer shelled 7th Battery O.P. in NEUVE CHAPELLE from direction of AUBERS Ridge.
4.p.m. RUE du BOIS shelled by PIPSQUEAK.
4.6.p.m. PIPSQUEAK had 3 direct hits on 7th Battery O.P.
4.10.p.m. and from)10.5 a.m. fired about 15 rounds which fell close
4.30.p.m. to 5.15.p.m.)to PORT ARTHUR from direction of ILLIES.
)PIPSQUEAK assisted also.

2. INFORMATION

LOCOMOTIVE:- 8.p.m. a train was heard moving somewhere behind HAUTE POMMERAU. Sounded to be going very slowly.
ENTANGLEMENTS:- At point 131 there is a permanent gap in the wire, about 5 feet wide. Enemy were mending wire round this point last night.
BOMBS:- At 12.20.p.m. a German aeroplane dropped a bomb 800 yards S. of the MEERUT Divisional Ammunition Column, wounding 2 women.
AIRCRAFT:- 11.35.a.m. AVIATIK sighted flying high between 11,000 and 12,000 feet, appeared from N.N.E. and travelled W. Identification marks black cross on white disc, giving appearance of rings at a distance. Engaged with 16 rounds, plane dropped suddenly after first round and then went on in a Westerly direction.

The cross
was
circular

Major R.A.

Brigade Major, Royal Artillery,
MEERUT DIVISION.

www.ingramcontent.com/pod-product-compliance
Lightning Source LLC
Chambersburg PA
CBHW081442160426
43193CB00013B/2363